Lost Traditions of
Celtic Shamanism

THE SIN EATER'S
Last Confessions

Ross Heaven

Llewellyn Publications
Woodbury, Minnesota

FIRST EDITION
First Printing, 2008

Book design by Rebecca Zins
Cover design by Gavin Dayton Duffy
Cover image © Lorry Eason/Digital Vision/Punchstock

Llewellyn is a registered trademark of Llewellyn Worldwide, Ltd.

Library of Congress Cataloging-in-Publication Data

Heaven, Ross.
    The sin eater's last confessions : lost traditions of Celtic shamanism / by Ross Heaven.
    —1st ed.
    p. cm.
    Includes index.
    ISBN 978-0-7387-1356-4
    1. Celts—Religion. 2. Shamanism. I. Title.
    BL900.H393 2008
    299'.16—dc22

                  2008014213

Llewellyn Publications
A Division of Llewellyn Worldwide, Ltd.
2143 Wooddale Drive, Dept. 978-0-7387-1356-4
Woodbury, MN 55125-2989, U.S.A.
www.llewellyn.com

Printed in the United States of America

For my children,
Mili, Jodie, Ocean, and Javen:
sin-free and perfect in every way.

Contents

Contents

DISCLAIMER

The techniques, recipes, and approaches in this book are for interest purposes only. The exercises presented here have been tested in many real-life applications, and no harm has ever arisen as a result (most people have benefited enormously). It is important, however, to act sensibly and responsibly when undertaking spiritual or emotional discovery work of any kind. It is also important that you double-check all formulas and recipes given in this book for legality and safety before using them internally or externally and, if you are in any doubt about any of these practices or recipes, that you take medical or other advice to reassure yourself that there are no contraindications.

Any application of these exercises is at the reader's own risk, and the author and publisher disclaim any liability arising directly or indirectly from them, their use, or the recipes described herein.

IN THE COUNTY of Hereford was an old Custom at Funerals, to hire poor people who were to take upon them all the Sins of the party deceased . . . These were called Sin Eaters.

The manner was that when a Corpse was brought out of the house and laid on the Bier; a Loaf of bread was brought out and delivered to the Sin-eater over the corpse, as also a Mazer-bowl full of beer, which he was to drink up, and sixpence in money, in consideration whereof he took upon him all the Sins of the Defunct, and freed him (or her) from Walking after they were dead.

John Aubrey, *Remains of Gentilism*, 1688[1]

---

1   An interesting reference source for this is "All Soul's Day & The Wild Horde," by Waverly
    Fitzgerald at www.schooloftheseasons.com (the direct link is http://www.schoolofthe
    seasons.com/allsouls.html, current as of March 24, 2008), which also describes the tra-
    dition of "going from house to house, gathering ingredients for soul-cakes. Sometimes
    these were left out for the poor to eat, sometimes given to the priest to pay for Masses for
    the souls of the dead; sometimes they were given to those professionals who took on the
    sins of the dead."

❧ ABHORRED BY THE superstitious villagers as a thing unclean, the sin-eater cut himself off from all social intercourse with his fellow creatures by reason of the life he had chosen; he lived as a rule in a remote place by himself, and those who chanced to meet him avoided him as they would a leper.

This unfortunate was held to be the associate of evil spirits, and given to witchcraft, incantations and unholy practices; only when a death took place did they seek him out, and when his purpose was accomplished they burned the wooden bowl and platter from which he had eaten the food handed across, or placed on the corpse for his consumption ...

Traces of this revolting cult are still to be found, but its roots are deeply buried in antiquity.

Bertram S. Puckle, *Funeral Customs:*
Their Origin and Development, 1926[2]

---

2   For more information on practices of honoring the dead, see *Funeral Customs: Their Origin and Development* by Bertram S. Puckle, published by T. Werner Laurie, 1926, and available online at http://www.sacredtexts.com/etc/fcod/fcod00.htm (current as of March 24, 2008).

❧ THE CUSTOM OF sin eating ... An old Celtic tradition that may still happen back in these mountains ... Somebody dies, and a meal is laid out, with an extra portion placed directly on the coffin. The real purists put the food right on the dead person's skin and make sure water and salt are part of the meal.

There's feasting all round, but all stops when the sin eater arrives. He/she is usually a person not quite whole in body or in mind, but there's a job to be done and a ritual to be consummated. He goes to the coffin ... mumbles a prayer ... and eats. The sin eater symbolically consumes the sins of the dead person, so the spirit can rest in peace.

This is vicarious atonement—whether it comes once a year or once in a lifetime or once and for all—the idea that responsibility can be delegated, that someone else, some sin eater or scapegoat—or savior—can absorb your personal faults. It's only a tiny step to believing somebody else, some scapegoat, can be held responsible for the evils of the world.

Sermon by the Reverend Dr. Maureen Killoran,
Unitarian Universalist Church of Asheville,
September 30, 2002

1

The Gateway to the Garden

... He comes, the human child
To the waters and the wild.
With a faery, hand in hand,
For the world's more full of weeping
than he can understand.

W. B. Yeats,
"The Stolen Child"

HEREFORD IS A Cathedral City—which really means nothing these days. It is another country town struggling to be modern, corporate, and accepted, with the same shops, culture, and concerns of any other town in England.

In 1968, though, when I moved there as a boy, it hadn't quite woken up to the modern world and still slept an ancient rural slumber, where myth and magic flowed through the landscapes of its strange Celtic dreams. The cathedral stood at its center, looking out over white- and black-beamed cottages and quirky alleyways, thin and winding, which led to curiosities and mysteries.

Among the town's more famous remembered citizens was Nell Gwynne, whose tiny cottage, easily missed in a row of look-alike dwellings, squeezed itself into one of these alleys.

An impoverished "orange girl," selling fruit to theatergoers—or, according to others, a child prostitute—Nell was born to the town in 1650. By the age of fifteen, she was an actress herself, although she may have been more courtesan than artist (when asked for her profession one day, Nell described herself not as an actress but as a "Protestant whore"). Three years later, regardless, she was the lover of Charles II, bearing him two illegitimate sons, whom she called the "little bastards."

Despite all of this, her rags-to-riches story was still celebrated in Hereford, along with her unconventional way of achieving fame.

Her life created something of a blueprint or a journeyman's map for how one could escape one's fate: by using creativity, guile, and, to its fullest advantage, whatever gift that God had bestowed on you, even if it was only the ability to catch the eye of royal blood.

No matter how slim a chance, such talents offered the possibility of escape from a town that, enclosed by hills and rivers, felt imprisoned, surrounded by natural walls and under scrutiny from the ghosts of the landscape itself. Perhaps the claustrophobia of this landscape accounted for the sense one had in Hereford of always being watched by some invisible force, and of the town's almost tangible desire to take a long-frustrated breath.

A river ran through it, snaking like a question mark—a fitting image since this river is called the Wye, its name an echo of the seeking-after-purpose that characterized the town itself and its people. It was a place in transition: backward-looking and caught in its web of history, but squinting into the future, unsure of what it would become as rumors of revolution and new values began to breach its city walls from an England poised for change and social upheaval. The people of the town were restless, not quite knowing which way to go, but anxious to begin their journey anyway after so many years of sleepwalking its streets.

Despite the developments taking place—"the red brick skin disease," as D. H. Lawrence called it, of look-alike newly built homes being pasted onto the landscape and layered on top of the black and white—it was two buildings, or, rather, their contents and what they represented, that summed up the mood of the town, telling the people what to believe about their world: the museum and the cathedral.

In pride of place in Hereford Museum was a small effigy, a figure of a man or woman bound with the words of a curse. It was found in the town in 1960, the year of my birth, but dates back hundreds of years before that. It was thought to have been used to ruin the crops of an enemy—one of the standard methods of agricultural rivalry and witchcraft in rural villages. The words of its curse read:

> *I act this spell upon you from my whole heart,*
> *wishing you to never rest*
> *nor eat nor sleep*
> *for the restern part of your life*

Words that showed, perhaps, just how effective such magic can be, for the town itself was asleep but not sleeping, exactly as the curse had hoped for: a somnambulist lost in a maze of time that was neither the future nor the past but the betwixt-and-between of an undefined now.

The museum stands a few hundred feet from the cathedral, the juxtaposition seeming in some subtle way to capture the strange duality of the town, where paganism and Craft-based magic rub shoulders with a Christianity that is really a surface veneer. This pagan Christianity is there in the cathedral as well, leading to the odd blurring of beliefs that is typical of the Celtic way, where the old gods wear Christian robes as nature spirits dance their way through churches like invisible currents of wind.

Should your journeys ever take you to this cathedral, for example, and you enter through the Castle Green, you will pass the site of a spring—Saint Ethelbert's Well—which, you will be told, sprang magically from the ground when Ethelbert's dead body touched it en route to its interment and the coffin-bearers rested awhile. Offa, King of the Mercians, had betrayed Ethelbert's love for his daughter, the princess, by having the saint's head cut from his body, and the waters of Hereford now flow with Ethelbert's tears.

There is a further shrine in the cathedral's north transept, named after another saint, Thomas de Cantilupe, the Bishop of Hereford from 1275–1282, which is also the site of miracles, including seventy cases of the dead being returned to life through contact with Thomas's relics and bones. Even Christian saints are Old World magicians in Hereford.

My family had recently moved from a city many miles away to a village just outside the town. Called Ullingswick, it is mentioned in the Domesday Book of 1086 as Ullingwic, the name deriving from "Ulla's Wick," *wick* being an Anglo-Saxon corruption of the Roman *viscus*, "a place of significance."

According to archeological studies, an early timber castle, known as Dunder Camp, stood to the north of the village, alongside our house, an old stone cottage called Harry's Croft, which dated from at least the 1600s.

Its name was a coincidence, since my father was also called Harry, and a *croft* is a dwelling place. Perhaps coincidence is not the right word, however. My father felt, instead, that the house had been calling him, across time and space, to live there, as he had before in some previous life when he had first given it its name.

The original cottage, along with the village school and its only shop, are all gone now, although Ullingswick remains, as it always has been, an agricultural community where nature guides the day, the moon shapes the nights, and the ghosts of Dunder Camp still move about the fields.

It was as if time slowed down in this village, altered its course, or ran backwards as it wished, moving at the pace and rhythm of the wind in the trees and grass. The rivers, forests, and hills were alive and whispering their secrets.

Strange things happened in this threshold place where the world of spirit met the landscape of the physical, as though there was a symbol, a metaphor, or a myth to be uncovered behind every seeming fact.

It is in this spiritually loaded place that the story of this book really begins.

At the edge of the village, alone and isolated from the rest of the community, there was a small cottage, long fallen into disrepair. I would pass it some days on my walks and grew curious about this mysterious building, whose lopsided architecture had begun to take on the form of the land itself. It stood at a crossroads, just back from the lane, surrounded by tall bushes and trees and fronted by a tangle of blackthorn and briars. It was a walk of about a mile from my own cottage, which was closer to the center of the village, and there were no other houses near it.

It had an atmosphere or personality of its own, this tumbling, whitewashed shack, like the fairy-tale cottage of a witch—something almost alive—and it snared my imagination.

Whenever I asked about it, however, or about who might live in such a twisted house, I was always met with silence or else warned to stay away. But village whispers are jungle drums, and it didn't take long for me to learn that the place was owned by a madman, a loner, someone "not like us," although no reasons were ever given to explain these apparent truths.

It was with these thoughts in mind one summer's day that I stood looking at this cottage. It seemed curious, given the asymmetry of the building and its unkempt appearance, that the garden, in parts at least, looked cared for.

But even that was strange. There were no flower beds as such; in fact, there were hardly any flowers at all. Instead, what I took to be weeds grew alongside more recognizable plants, all of them laid out in semi-ordered rows, as if the gardener had intended to grow weeds and given them as much care and attention as everything else.

Just as I thought that, a movement caught my eye, and I turned back to the house, coming face-to-face for the first time with the occupant of this strange-looking dwelling: the madman himself.

In a matter of instants, while my attention had been taken by the curiosity of his garden, the madman had silently left his cottage and crossed the land between us. Now we were separated just by his unkempt hedge.

"There are no such things as weeds," he said. These were the first words I heard him speak, and they stayed with me because just moments before I had been wondering the same thing as

I looked at the arrangement of plants in his garden: what *is* a weed?

To me, the madman seemed ancient, but later I would learn that he was in his sixties when I met him and, with the benefit of passing time, I would say now that he was a young sixty who would pass for a man in his fifties or even his forties with a little attention to his appearance. But it was evident that vanity was not his way.

He was dressed oddly for the times (the late 1960s). While everyone else in the village wore farm overalls or jeans—the ubiquitous new fashion style—he seemed overdressed in a white collarless shirt, black trousers, and waistcoat. To enhance the effect, a gold fob-watch hung from the pocket of his waistcoat. He wore no shoes, however, or anything else on his feet.

A shock of hair fell over his grey-blue eyes, and his features were tight, not loose with age. I imagine he would have been handsome in his youth.

"What is a weed, after all?" he said to my unstated question; "A weed is simply a gift from nature that we don't care to receive. Would you like to come in and see?"

His hand was on the gate, and I would like to say that I stepped through it without hesitation and across the threshold between us in one magical movement. The truth, however, is that my curiosity battled for a few moments against uncertainty,

s, and even a little fear, after all I had been told about this
cottage and its unusual owner. I didn't even know his
name.

"Adam," he said, stretching out his hand to shake mine.

The mystery was too thick, the adventure too rich to leave
by now, so, despite my reservations, I shook his hand, and I did
cross that threshold. It was the beginning of a friendship that
was to last from my childhood to my adult years, although it is
only now, more than thirty years later, that I realize the full implications of the time we spent together and the wisdom that Adam
had to teach. And so it is only now that I can keep my promise to
Adam to make his confession by the telling of his life.

As I grew to know Adam, it became clear why he lived as he
did, where he did, and why he was regarded warily by others, for
in his younger days, Adam had been a sin eater (*bwytawr pechod*
in the Welsh, from which this tradition comes)—a devourer of
human sins—and his was a story of the soul, what it may contain, and how it can be healed and find purpose.

These are still subjects rarely considered in mainstream life,
subjects regarded as fear-filled and unnerving, in fact, since by
acknowledging the soul at all we must look into our own and see
what darkness it may hold.

During the time we spent together, Adam would teach me
some of these secrets: what the soul is, how we might know its

true intentions, and how sin can shape and corrupt it, as well as how it can be restored through spiritual practice and the power of confession, plants, rituals, and omens.

This book is a record of those teachings and how they might benefit us all so that the confusions of the world do not enter our hearts or become weights upon our souls, and so we can become happier, freer, and more certain of living our purpose.

Maybe every country and every village of the world has its Adam. If so, you will find him in some strange place beyond the boundaries of a town whose very reason for existence seems to be the asking of a question. His life will be a whispered secret, and he will act with a special knowingness that others will call madness or eccentricity. He will tell you that the veil between worlds is thinner than you have been led to believe.

Those who find the sin eater will leave their encounter with a sense of the strangeness of life and the realization that there are things that move in darkness which influence all who walk in sunlight. If chance should take you to a meeting of this kind, you will understand the meaning of your soul.

2

The Spirit of the Plants

That garden sweet, that lady fair,
And all sweet shapes and odours there,
In truth have never passed away;
'Tis we, 'tis ours, are changed; not they.

Percy Bysshe Shelley,
"The Sensitive Plant"

I HAD NEVER taken a great interest in plants. The cottage where I lived had a garden of about two acres, not big by country standards, where my father grew a mix of flowers and vegetables half-successfully, and where I sometimes pottered about with him on Saturday afternoons, both of us pretending we knew what we were doing as we watered and fertilized and cleared the odd stone from a row of cabbages or peas.

My father had been a city boy like me before we moved to the village, and neither of us really knew what a vegetable was. Where we came from, they were things that arrived in shops and you ate begrudgingly on Sundays and tried to avoid for the rest of the week.

With Adam, it was different. The way he spoke about plants as we meandered through his garden on the days that followed, every herb, flower, bush, and tree was alive and had a personality of its own. He seemed especially fond of weeds, those bothersome plants that my father and I spent our time pulling out of the vegetable patch and discarding.

"You see those," he said one day, pointing at a patch of nettles; "they are some of the most useful plants God gave us."

"Nettles?" I asked incredulously, since my father and I had just devoted days to getting rid of a patch so we could reclaim a little more of our land from the briars and thickets around it.

"You've still got the city in you," he laughed. "We'll have to get this modern ignorance out of you if you're going to learn anything about the real world.

"Every child of nature knows what nettles are good for—or at least they used to, before the city started making its way down here too," he added, glancing up at a distant line of pylons carrying electrical cables on a hill across the valley. "Metal trying to be trees," he muttered. Then, in a more upbeat tone: "Let me tell you what nettles can do."

He knelt next to the nettle patch and began whispering to them.

"What are you doing?" I asked.

"I'm asking permission," he said—then, before my next question, he added: "for this," as he grabbed a handful of nettles at mid-stalk and broke them off in his hand. I'd been stung by nettles before and knew that must have hurt, but he seemed completely unconcerned.

By now, I was quite used to Adam's ability to anticipate and answer my questions before they were even asked, so I wasn't surprised when he continued: "Like love and most things in life, the nettle only hurts when you touch it too lightly. When you commit to it, it commits to you.

"Of course, you'd better ask its permission first—and know when to let go as well! In plain language: grab the nettle firmly, and it will not sting.

"There is no better plant for healing the blood," he went on. "In the old days, people knew that blood is the juice of the soul. It is where our spirit lives. Problems with the blood therefore mean that our spirit is upset in some way, probably because another spirit is feeding from ours.

"The spirit of the nettle is a good one—an ally to human folk. Its job is to fight off bothersome spirits who want to take our power away. It will do that for you if you ask it, and any problems with the blood will then clear up. As a bonus," he added, almost in a stage whisper and with a sparkle in his eyes, "it is one of the best plants a lady can use if she wants a bigger bosom!

"In some parts of the world," he said, nodding at the Black Hills on the horizon, which are the border of Wales, "doctors sting their patients with nettles to purify the blood."

With that, he rolled up his sleeves and began to lightly run the nettles across his inner arm where it makes a crook at the elbow, then did the same with the backs of his knees. Almost immediately, the red bumps of nettle stings began to form.

"Bad spirits can live in the blood, but it's the angles and corners of the body where they most like to gather and hide—the elbows, knees, and other joints. When you sting those places it puts heat into them, and those spirits will rise to the surface to cool. Then you need only take a cold bath and use this little plant"—he pointed to a chamomile—"to wash off the infection from the surface of your skin. The water takes it away, back into the earth. Would you like to try them?"

"No, thank you!" I almost shouted.

"I said 'them'—the nettles—not 'it'—the stinging," he chuckled. "You can drink nettles in a tea as well—about half a cup of leaves with hot water and honey. Three cups a day for nine days, and you will be good as new." [1]

"How do you know all this?" I asked. I'd never seen or heard anything like that before.

"Ah, now you want the story of my life!" he said with a smile. "Well, come on in to the house, and we'll share some nettle tea, and I'll begin my confession!"

ADAM DILWYN VAUGHAN was born in Llanddewi Brefi, a small village in Ceredigion (Cardiganshire), in 1911. His last two names

---

1   For more information on nettles and their uses, see "Stinging Nettles" by Bob McBob, November 27, 2003, an article at the bbc.co.uk h2g2 website (reference: http://www.bbc.co.uk/dna/h2g2/A1310950, accessed March 24, 2008).

were of Celtic, pre-Christian origin. *Dilwyn* means "blessed" and "pure," from the Welsh words *dilys*, "genuine," and *gwyn*, "fair and white," while *Vaughan* is a descriptive name derived from the word *fychan*, which means "younger," and was used to distinguish father from son.

Why he was given the first name Adam was a mystery to him, although he understood that its origins were in the words for earth, man, or life. "A blessed and pure life for a man of the earth" was what he therefore took his name to mean and what he believed his parents wished for him.

Llanddewi Brefi—the English pronunciation is roughly "Hlan-thewi Brevvy"—was founded in the sixth century AD when Saint David, the patron saint of Wales, held the first synod there. The town still bears his name, *Llan* referring to a holy place and *ddewi* being a variant of the name David.

It is said that the ground miraculously rose up beneath the saint when he began to preach so he could be heard throughout the whole of Wales. He spoke of sins, redemption, and blessings, and encouraged those present to "do the little things that you have seen me do and heard about, and walk the path that our fathers have trod before us."

"Do the little things" (*Gwnewch y pethau bychain*) is still a well-used expression in Wales. It means to take action and express love, compassion, and spiritual purpose in *everything* that you do, instead of waiting to make big gestures or for moments that may never come. More mundanely, it means to live a sin-free life.

The church of Llanddewi Brefi is dedicated to Saint David and was built in the twelfth century at the place of his synod, although the site had been a center for worship since at least the seventh century, and fragments of much older buildings are incorporated into the church, which also houses some of the oldest religious artifacts in the United Kingdom. The community is rural, mostly based on farming. God-fearing notions of sin and the desire for salvation are part of the fabric of the town itself.

Adam was born the seventh in a family of nine children. His mother, Peg, had been what he called a "cunning woman." She knew the nature of herbs and how to cure illness among animals and people, and her services were much in demand by the community, who preferred to visit her than put its trust in doctors and veterinarians, who they saw as the purveyors of "newfangled science."

Adam would go for long walks with her during the spring and summer months, collecting plants and flowers for potions and creams. Then, during the autumn and winter, the kitchen would be filled with activity and the smells of herbs being prepared for storage; a cozy candlelit scene, as Adam recalled it, in contrast to the harsh weather that rolled in over the wild, darkened hills and battered the windows of their cottage. By the age of ten, Adam was as familiar with herbs as his mother and knew the causes and cures of disease as well as she did.

His father had an equal impact on young Adam and eventually influenced his choice of profession. Aneurin Vaughan (a name meaning "noble") was a farm laborer and in many ways a plain man. He had a keen interest in the Bible, however, and took to preaching, as well as to reading large tracts of the Testament to his children most evenings. His devotion was recognized by the church, and the congregation reacted fondly to his occasional warm sermons about love and the care of the soul.

There was another aspect to his work as well: with at least partial approval of the church, Aneurin was a sin eater.

Today, there is little known about this healing practice, and the last sin eaters were said to have died out in Wales in the 1850s. Aneurin and his son, who followed his father into the tradition, would beg to differ, however, as their own pastoral duties in this respect continued, though less formally and with waning approval from the church, well into the 1950s. It was then that Adam, after a lifetime in Wales, moved to Herefordshire, on the English side of the Welsh borders, and there the tradition is thought to have ended.

Adam believed he was the last sin eater, although this may not be strictly true. The shamans of many cultures practice a form of sin eating that is often called "soul retrieval" or "spirit extraction"—the removal of energies that can otherwise lead to illness, and the return of good energy to restore balance to the soul.

For most shamans, my later studies were to show me, the human body is comprised of energy, and it is this energy—formless, nameless, and shapeless in itself—that constitutes our lifeforce, or soul. For the sin eater, how we use (or lose) this energy is fundamental to who we are, and it is bound up in notions of guilt, shame, blame, retribution, and sin. The task of the sin eater, in common with all shamans, is to remove harmful energy (or "sin") and restore the patient to equilibrium through the practice of atonement—or, as Adam preferred to pronounce it, at-*one*-ment: a return to our original state of purity.

Adam knew little about sin eating outside of what he had learned first-hand of it, but according to him, it was an honorable profession and a healing tradition clearly derived from the Bible and the will of God. In Leviticus 14:21, for example, there is a reference to the "atonement" made by a priest on behalf of another, and to a "sin offering" made to free the sinner from blame.[2]

---

2   There are many translations and editions of the Bible, most of them saying the same thing in slightly different words. The one I own, and which I have referred to most often in this book, is *The Holy Bible*, Monsignor Knox translation of the Old Testament, with a preface by Cardinal Bernard Griffin, Archbishop of Westminster, 1954.

> ... the priest shall offer the sin offering, and make atonement for him who is to be cleansed from his uncleanness ...

Leviticus 16:21–22 and 16:26 also describe a "scapegoating" ritual, where, in a not dissimilar way, Aaron confessed the sins of the children of Israel on the Day of Atonement, above the head of a goat that was then sent into the wilderness bearing those sins and carrying them free of the people.

> He [Aaron] is to lay both hands on the head of the live goat and confess over it all the wickedness and rebellion of the Israelites—all their sins—and put them on the goat's head. He shall send the goat away into the desert in the care of a man appointed for the task. The goat will carry on itself all their sins to a solitary place; and the man shall release it in the desert ...

> The man who releases the goat as a scapegoat must wash his clothes and bathe himself with water; afterward he may come into the camp.

In its more recent form as a Celtic tradition, a sin eater would be employed by the family of a deceased person, or sometimes by the church, to eat a last meal (often just water and salt) from the belly of the corpse as it lay in state. By so doing he would absorb the sins of the dead and the deceased would have passage to the next world.

Traditionally, the sin eater was given a few coins for his trouble but other than that was avoided "like the plague" by the community he served, who regarded him as sin-filled and unclean as a result of his work, although this seems to have not been the case for Aneurin Vaughan. For others, however, and in Adam's life more obviously, it was almost as if an unwritten contract existed between the healer and the community that they would not meet outside of the therapeutic environment. That is why sin eaters lived at the edge of the village and children were warned away from them.

Sin eaters rarely worked just with the dead, however. Many of them, because of their rural location and their closeness to nature—which they regarded as "the visible face of spirit"—were also skilled in folk medicine.

Folk medicine can be described as a form of "root doctoring," or herbalism, that works with the medicinal properties and the spiritual essence of plants—never one without the other. Thus, Adam knew that nettles could be used for spiritual cleansing just as they could for more physical purposes, such as alleviating skin problems, rheumatism, and arthritis—as well as increasing the breast size of a young lady.[3]

---

3   The University of Plymouth in England has recently proved that nettles do indeed have benefits for arthritis sufferers, confirming folk law dating back to Roman times, which stated that flogging with nettles (urtication) would cure chronic rheumatism. For more information on this and other uses of nettles, see the BBC h2g2 website at http://www.bbc.co.uk/dna/h2g2/A1310950.

Another example was vervain. A tonic made from this plant would help to cure depression, paranoia, and insomnia; all symptoms, as Adam saw it, of guilt or shame—an emotional reaction brought about by the intrusive spirit of sin.

For a similar reason, therefore, the plant could also be used as a charm for protection from sin and to drive away "evil spirits." Its latter use had nothing to do with biochemistry or herbalism per se, but with the spiritual intention of the plant, and to use it in this way, the healer had to know the purpose of its soul.

By the same token, marigolds can be used to treat skin rashes, inflammations, and ulcers (symptoms, again, of sin in the form of bodily reactions to an intrusive energy), but they will also soothe and calm the spirit. The thirteenth-century herbalist Aemilius Macer knew this, too, and wrote that marigold flowers have the power to draw "wicked humours out."

The entirety, almost, of Adam's life had been spent, in one way or another, healing and nurturing the soul. Which, one day, brought me to the question: what exactly *is* the soul?

It was a question which Adam characteristically answered by making me discover it for myself through the truths of the natural world.

3

The Soul of
the Great Tree

❖ The trees are coming into leaf
Like something almost being said;
The recent buds relax and spread,
Their greenness is a kind of grief.

Philip Larkin,
"The Trees"

In 1921, in Hereford, Alfred Watkins had a sudden realization— "a flood of ancestral memory," he called it—that certain places, such as standing stones, sacred trees, burial mounds, and cathedrals, fell in straight lines for miles, and that they were somehow connected by an invisible network of soul and spirit.

As he stood on a Herefordshire hill one day, he suddenly saw what had always been there, but so obvious and familiar that it had been hidden from his eyes: a trackway across the land of energy routes to which human beings had always been drawn, unconsciously, to build their monuments and places of rest. He wrote of this in his book *The Old Straight Track*, which was the first time the world would hear of ley lines.[4]

Hereford has many such lines, like a web of energy laid across the land, all of them messengers of the deeper spirit that moves within the earth and the sanctity of certain natural places of power.

"Most gardens are an aberration," said Adam one day. "Nature rarely needs a manicure. When we tidy things up, we forget what they are and we try to make them a part of *our* world instead of recognizing the truth: that we are a part of nature. Not *apart*, but *a part*.

---

4   For information on Watkins and ley lines, see Alfred Watkins, *The Old Straight Track: The Classic Book on Ley Lines*, published by Abacus (1994).

"Every garden is actually a pharmacy when left to its own devices—did you know that? And every one of these plants has a purpose. When we chop them down and tidy them up, we deny ourselves their healing.

"Take this plant—Good Saint John (St. John's Wort)—named after the Baptist," he said, pointing to a clump of tall, spindly plants with bright yellow flowers. "It will help you dream and comfort you from nightmares. It will heal your stomach, strengthen your back, and protect you from shock. The flowers of this plant are the best defense there is against witchcraft and 'unwelcome guests'—phantoms. Its other name, *hypericum*, means 'power over apparitions.' All of this from one simple plant that most people would tidy up and throw away.

"Or take this one—thyme. Its name means 'fumigation,' and if you burn it and stand in its smoke, it will cleanse you and take away all sadness and confusion. Or, if you make a tea of it with honey and lemon, there is no finer cure for sore throats and coughs. In this way, all plants have a job to do on the body and on the spirit.

"The nettles we drink in our tea—I bet your father curses them and tries to get rid of them wherever they grow, doesn't he?" I smiled because of course he did.

"Nettles have a poor reputation, but they are one of our finest allies for healing the blood and contacting the ... fairy world," he said after a slight pause. "You believe in fairies, don't you?"

I had no idea if I did or not. Apart from the famous photographs of the Cottingley Fairies,[5] published in 1920 and widely regarded as innocent fakes, I had only ever seen fairies in picture books and never really considered if I believed these images to be based in any kind of fact. But I nodded out of politeness anyway.

"Good. You should. And one day I will show you how to call them. Nettles are quite exceptional for raising the heat of the body, which is necessary for seeing the fairy world. Roman soldiers bought their own nettles with them when they came to our land and used to rub them on their skin to keep out the British cold—but I don't know whether they saw the fey folk as a consequence!

"They heat you up, you see, and when they touch your skin, they change the way you look at the world. If you've been stung by a nettle, you'll know what I mean. No matter where you were stung, you will have felt a buzzing in your head and a strange sensation at the back of your neck, near your shoulders, yes?"

This time I nodded with more conviction, having experienced exactly what he was talking about when I had been stung in the past.

---

5   For information on the Cottingley Fairies and photographs of the fairies themselves, see www.cottingley.net. The direct link is http://en.wikipedia.org/wiki/Cottingley_Fairies, and was current as of March 24, 2008.

"That sensation has nothing to do with the nettles; it's because the spirits grow near and begin to speak to your soul."

"What *is* the soul?" I asked. In my world—the world of most city kids and most Westerners, in fact—the soul was a matter of fancy, not fact. Who had ever seen a soul, after all?

Adam seemed pleased with the question. "Excellent!" he said, clapping his hands together. "Now we can go for a walk!"

"But..."

"Don't worry; we'll answer your question all right, but we need to take a walk to do it. And I need to tell you about trees: some of the most important people alive."

Adam set off across the fields at the slowest pace imaginable, like a walking meditation. "This is the way to walk when you are hunting the soul," he said.

"Always at the pace of nature. And how do you know what that is? Watch the wind in the trees, the clouds in the sky, or the speed at which a stream flows: that is nature's pace. Keep to that, and breathe deeply.

"Keep your eyes on the ground as well and try to walk in my footsteps if you can. When you do that, your senses will open and you'll see things you've never seen before."

After about fifteen minutes of this walking at the pace of nature, I began to understand what he meant. Something *did* start to change in me, and I found myself noticing things I'd never paid attention to before.

Firstly, there was a sort of sheen to the earth, as if there was a layer of energy or mist between me and the ground. With it, the world became silent except when I took my attention to certain sounds; then the only thing in the world became the music of the wind, or the rustle of leaves, or the gurgle of the stream to my right, and all of it seemed to have a new depth, as if layers of voices—the water, wind, and leaves—were communicating with each other and with me. I became, I suppose, hypnotized, enchanted by the realization that nature was alive and was talk-ing to me.

And then a sort of fear arose as I noticed where I was placing my feet. If nature was alive, then this grass I was stepping on was being killed by my clumsy actions. I tried to step only on soil after that, but even as my foot was in mid-air I realized that the soil also contained life in the form of microorganisms as well as the insects that scurried away as the shadow of my foot approached their world. I became clumsy and increasingly uncomfortable with my newfound understanding that I was a sort of walking death machine: each time I moved, something died.

At that moment, a gust of wind came out of nowhere and hit me in the back. I felt the jolt of it and, along with it, a new realization: that all of nature was like this. The wind blew the leaves from the trees, the sun dried them, the rain made them mulch, and this fed the earth, giving rise to the life I had become destroyer of. All things were connected and equally important in nature, if only as food for the earth from which the trees and their leaves would grow. I would die one day too and feed the insects whose lives I took now. Natural justice, I supposed.

There was sacrifice in everything, a cycle to it all—matter becoming spirit and spirit becoming matter—and a kind of beauty and fairness. Everything was as it was meant to be: the only way it *could* be when we see ourselves as part of nature. With this I began to relax, going deeper into mindlessness, without need of thoughts at all.

At some point in this relaxed state, I noticed that Adam was talking quietly to me about trees.

"They all contain mystery. Take the simple apple tree. We know it for its fruit, but the old ones—the doctors who cared for the people before the doctors came[6]—knew that the apple tree was also a shelter for lunatics: people who see the divine in all things.

---

6   Adam often spoke of "the old ones," "the old ways," and "the doctors who cared for the people before the doctors came." By these references he meant traditional practitioners and practices, pagan in origin, which made use of folkways and natural medicines to tend to the physical and spiritual health of the people of Wales.

"It was, after all, the original tree of Eden, which brought knowledge of good and evil. Those who wanted to know these things for themselves would sit and dream beneath apple trees and open themselves to the world of the soul, which is nature in all its forms and all the cycles of the earth.

"Silence, breath, the stillness of nature, and the presence of the tree are the ingredients for alchemy, just as Eve and the Buddha found, there in the shade of a tree. Trees can tell us all we need to know about truth, though it may take us a lifetime or two to realize that, because they move and speak so much slower than us!

"The birch tree is another messenger. It is the first tree of the old language,[7] and it stands for new beginnings and the ability to develop magic.

"The hazel is the tree of poets, and if you chew its fruits you will gain the power of inspiration. You have heard of 'witch hazel'? It is so-called because it is where witches and wizards gain their understanding.

---

7   "The old language" is a reference to the "tree language" of the Ogham, which, according to legend, was invented soon after the fall of the Tower of Babel. Its alphabet is based on the names of trees, and it has been known as a "tree alphabet" since around the tenth century. Thus, the letters of the old language are *beith*, which means "birch tree," *luis*, which means "rowan," *fearn*, which means "alder," *sail*, which means "willow," and so on. Ogham inscriptions are found in Wales and Ireland, and tend to be used on territory markers and gravestones. For more information, see http://www.omniglot.com. The direct link, http://www.omniglot.com/writing/ogham.htm, was current as of March 24, 2008.

"If you should meet with the hawthorn during your travels, however, it is time to be cautious and find another route. Its gift is to warn you of troubles to come.

"Holly can be like that too. It stands for life, death, and rebirth—the whole cycle of nature, which is greater than our minds can comprehend. That is why, if you spend too long with holly, it will leave you disoriented. If that is ever the case for you, seek out the rowan—the mountain ash—which will give you the concentration and focus you need to find your way again. Its job is to ward off unhelpful energies, which is why, in the old days, farmers made fences of rowan to protect their cattle so they grew fat and thrived.

"How did the old ones know so much about trees? The answer is simple: they asked the spirit of the tree, and it told them. Trees are so much more self-aware than human beings, you see. They know what they are here to do, and because they are bigger than us and have lived longer, they have a loftier understanding and a more timeless perspective on life. By spending time with trees—speaking with them and noting what they do, where they grow, how they appear—you get a sense of their purpose and your own, and a new perspective on both of your lives.

"Take the willows we just passed, for example. What is their 'purpose'? Well, they grow on the banks of the stream, where the spirit of water meets the spirit of the land: a betwixt-and-between place, a threshold, a shadowland. Their purpose, therefore, is to offer a gateway between one world and the next, which is why, incidentally, they are often planted in graveyards. Of course, no follower of any newfangled religion these days knows why we plant willows in cemeteries, and if they did, they would probably be scared to death, because no good Christian believes in the spirits anymore. It is against their religion! But that is the reason: willow trees are our guardians and gateways.

"And notice that they grow near water, so they must have strong foundations. This, then, is another of their gifts: they teach us to endure, to be strong and grounded. Whenever life knocks you around, find yourself a willow to sit by, and it will whisper to your dreams and give you the strength you need."

Adam's sermon on trees was delivered in a monotone semi-whisper, and it felt as if I was not absorbing information directly through his words but in a subliminal way, so I understood what he was saying without entirely hearing what he had said. His next words were more commanding, however.

"Lift up your eyes," he said. "You wanted to know about the soul, and this is where we find out."

I looked up and saw that we were standing in a large field of straw, cornstalks left from an earlier harvest. Its gold stretched from hedgerow to hedgerow as far as the eye could see. At its center stood an oak tree, huge and powerful, its branches spanning the sky, some of them with bright ribbons hanging from them and dancing in the breeze; its roots snaking deep into the earth, and its center gnarled and strong. Its very middle was missing, however, as if blasted away, and there was a hole like a cave in its trunk.

"The holy oak, the most beloved tree of all. It stands for divine spirit and the powers of sky and earth. Its name in the old language is *Arddam*—same as me, though spelt a little differently! *Arddam Dossa* to be precise, which means 'most exalted of trees,' the 'protecting chief.' The oak is the protector of the land and will give you shelter, serenity, and guidance, since you, too, were born from the soil.

"This one is even more special. You see that its center is missing? That is because it was struck by lightning a few years ago now, which is a mark of honor that only the most powerful and worthy of trees receive. It means that this tree was chosen as a messenger of spirit, and it can enlighten us, too, if we choose to meet that spirit."

Adam then gave me instructions for how to meet the spirit it contained: by walking at the pace of nature towards the tree, paying close attention to it until I felt a change in the air around me. I was then to sit down in front of the oak. The change in the air came about twenty feet from the trunk.

"Most people move too fast to notice that change," said Adam. "But it's always there. It is a change in the nature of things. Trees are our great transformers. They take the pollution and toxins we humans create and turn it back into oxygen. Their overriding gift to us is life: the very air that we breathe. What you felt was a shift in energy and a slight coolness as you entered the purer air surrounding the tree. Now you can experience real, fresh oxygen! Let your eyes go out of focus as you look at the tree, and tell me what you see."

What I saw as I sat quietly, filling my lungs with fresh air and feeling the sun on my back, was a shimmering around the tree, like the sheen from the earth I had seen earlier, then small particles of light that coalesced around the trunk and became waves. It was as if the tree had a glow to it, expanding outwards on all sides to create a pool of hazy grey-blue light: the soul of the tree.

The shimmering light was drawn into and out of the hole in the trunk, as if the tree was itself breathing, and my eyes followed its breath into the darkness of the cave at its center.

This hole suddenly seemed very inviting, and I stood up and walked towards it, then backed in and sat down as the trunk enfolded me. I closed my eyes, and pictures began to form of what the tree must have seen down the ages: images of nature and man and time and change, all of it spiralling like circles. I felt myself drifting off and upwards, following the spirals through the trunk, the branches, and the leaves of the oak, becoming mist-like myself and entering the sky, moving away from Earth and into a world of dancing stars.

There was a cloud within the stars, a fog of energy that was crackling and sparking like the flash of ideas across the synapses of the brain in the maps I have subsequently seen of minds creating thought. Beyond it there were what appeared to be giant spiderwebs like perverse stars, each one holding the grey and lifeless form of a man or woman suspended in space. The human webs made a cordon around the energy-cloud.

The cloud intrigued me and seemed incredibly attractive somehow, as if radiating peace and benign intelligence. I tried to steer myself towards it but managed only to drift towards one of the webs that hung between me and it. I began to panic. I did not want to become trapped there along with those other tortured forms. I can't remember whether I cried out, but suddenly Adam's hand grabbed me and pulled me bodily from the trunk.

"That's enough!" he said sharply. Then, in a gentler tone as I opened my eyes: "Trees are transformers, as I said. They can transform us, too, and take us into the world of spirit before our time. There is an hour in everyone's life for their visit to *annwyn*, the otherworld, but, for most, it is at the moment of death, *not* in the midst of their young lives!"

Then, softening his tone again, he added: "Let's call today the beginning of your understanding of the soul. There will be time for questions later."

With that, he reached into the tree and took some of the soot that the lightning had left on the trunk and rubbed it on my face.

"Now you are skin-covered lightning!" he said. "This soot is a blessing. The old ones knew the power of lightning, and to protect their young and help them grow in power and wisdom, they would find a tree like this and smear their children's faces with this soot. It'll help your soul stay in your body!"

With that, we took our slow walk back across the fields to Adam's cottage as the sun warmed away my shivers.

4

The Web of Dreams and Lies

A fool sees not the same tree
that a wise man sees.
He whose face gives no light
shall never become a star.

William Blake,
"Proverbs of Hell"

THE SOUL, IN sin-eating practice, is the energy field that surrounds, encapsulates, and suffuses all living things—a human being just as much as a tree.

Following my experience with the oak, I found that I could see this energy around most things: a leaf, a dog, a person, the outline of the distant hills as they touched the sky. All things have a soul, and this soul is easily seen by slowing down to the pace of nature, breathing deeply and evenly, and allowing our gaze to become soft so we are not staring *at* something but merging *with* it. By doing so, we begin to perceive an uncommon reality and the invisible world makes itself known.

In Adam's tradition, this was known as "dreaming it [reality] into being"—seeing reality, that is, in a new way—since the experience, from a human perspective, is very like dreaming but with one's eyes still open. We are in a relaxed, almost drowsy state, and, in this condition, we are in closer contact with the imaginative and creative parts of ourselves that the rush and distractions of modern life usually make unavailable to us. Mostly, it is about slowing down and paying attention. When we do so, we see things we have not noticed before—including the presence of a soul.

Being able to see the glow of the soul does not explain its nature, however, and this was something I needed to explore more deeply with Adam. Our conversations led to some surprises.

For one thing, in sin-eating tradition, human beings are not believed to be born with souls—not, at least, in the way we have come to understand them through mainstream religions—but must develop or "earn" them through their actions. The quality and nature of each person's soul is therefore a reflection of the life they have led and the experiences they have absorbed. From the size and density of the energy fields around us, it is possible to tell what sort of lives we have lived.

"All parents know that their newborn does not have a soul and is not fully present in the world," said Adam, as if this was common knowledge. "Babies are dreamers, still attached to the spirit from which they were born, and there is an ethereal quality to them. In fact, ethereal—'as light as air'—is a good word for it. Newborns are creatures of air, and it may be months or years before they have a sense of Earth about them.

"During these months, if a parent looks carefully above the head of his sleeping child, he may see the cord of light that still connects his child to the spirit world. This will gradually fade when the child finds the nugget of its soul and makes the decision to stay with us on Earth. Then that soul has the *potential* to grow, but it does not fully form until around the age of twenty-one, which is why we call it a 'coming of age.'"

Only at the age of twenty-one, I later learned, does an adult develop the capacity for abstract thought, and through this for the evolution of a personal ethical code, or what we might call "the makings of a soul."

Before that, children exhibit what scientists call "magical thinking": the assumption that, because they believe something, it is automatically real—like when a child imagines that because he did not mean to hurt his brother, his brother was not hurt by his kick or punch, or that because he hides beneath a blanket, the world really has gone away and the angry parent has vanished.

To counter this (and because they have lost the capacity for magical thinking themselves), most parents teach their children about the world in concrete terms and with black-and-white examples of "right" and "wrong."

During our early years, we are therefore forming a *foundation* for our souls through what we learn from others—but it is not until we "come of age" that the voyage of our own souls can truly begin, because then we are capable of greater abstraction and become seekers after our own truths, discovering right and wrong for ourselves. It is at this point that we really begin to build a soul through our choices and personal actions.

"We are born with an energy that foreshadows our soul to come, just as a seed foreshadows a flower," Adam explained. "But only by that seed finding ways to nurture itself—with sunlight and rain and healthy soil—can it become the brightest and best of flowers as it intended itself to be.

"Some seeds find their purpose and the ground to support them; some fall on barren land and when the rains come, they rot. Most fall to average soil and, in that way, compromise their potential, because an average flower can only ever result from average soil. So it is with us: if we give ourselves to the average and not the exceptional, we never fully become what we could or what we intended for ourselves.

"The most basic purpose of a flower is to be fully a part of life; for example, to be bright, beautiful, and attractive to the creatures that feed from it, shelter beneath it, live within it, or carry its seeds to other gardens so that life itself is celebrated. So, again, is it with us. When we compromise our soul's purpose, we remove ourselves from life. We all have a duty, therefore—*to life itself*—to stay true to the purpose of our souls."

But how do we know the purpose of our souls, I wondered, beyond the purpose we all have of being "fully a part of life"— that is, of living?

"In my work, I have been blessed—and cursed—to meet many souls, and to know the place from which all souls are born," said

Adam. "I conceive of it like this: there is a cloud of awareness somewhere out there"—he nodded to the sky—"made up of what we might call spiritual intelligence; the essence of every living thing. It is one energy made up of many individual energies; a community of purpose—just as a single flower may contain hundreds of seeds but is still one flower, with every part precisely and perfectly what it was created to be.

"The mood of that cloud of awareness—the feeling it evokes when we meet it—is one of peace and love and perfection. It is this cloud that we occupy as spirit and that we are born from, and so I conclude that love and perfection is also the natural state of every human being, which is revealed in the bliss of a newborn child.

"When you decided to leave that cloud and drift free like a seed on the wind, you carried that same mood and potential with you, and you also had a reason or purpose to leave that community. Why else would you go?

"Each of us needs to know what our purpose was—and is. It might be to remind the world of love and show them that it is possible, or it might be far more mundane than that: to become a gardener and get your hands dirty like me, perhaps! After all, it is wonderful to be a cloud, but a cloud is not a man, with a body, a story to tell, or experiences to share and take back with him when he returns to that community of souls. Your underlying purpose in being born, then, was to test your love and knowledge in the garden of flesh and deeds, which is this world.

"But it would be very boring, wouldn't it, if each of us came here with a mission and simply fulfilled it? Where would be the fun in that! And what would it teach us?

"And so we remember to forget when we leave that cloud of awareness so that our journeys here on Earth sing to our souls and do not bore us as, in one way or another, we play out the purpose we chose.

"By the time we die, through the fullness of our experience, we all have the soul we deserve, and this is the energy we use to make our great journey back to the community from which we came—if we are lucky, that is."

As so often happened when we touched on matters of the soul, Adam's words became more poetic and cryptic as my questions became more direct and pragmatic. I had challenged him on this before, and his answer had been that he was not here to teach me anything and "certainly I'm not speaking to your mind! The language of the soul is poetry, metaphor, symbol, and dreams, and it is your soul that needs to wake up and remember its purpose. If I just give you answers, they would be eaten up by your mind and filed away as 'unimportant.' Not only would they mean nothing to you, but you wouldn't believe them anyway, because they would be *my* answers, not *yours*! And so I plant seeds. It is up to you if and how you grow flowers."

This time I really wanted to understand, however, so I pushed him for more. "What do you mean that 'in one way or another' we play out our purpose? And that 'if we are lucky' our souls return to where they came from?" I asked—and for once, to my surprise, Adam was more forthcoming.

"Your father is the manager of an insurance company, isn't he?"

I nodded. I'd told Adam before about the reason for our move to the country—my father's promotion within his firm—and a little about my family.

"Your father was the eldest of thirteen—a working-class boy like me," said Adam. "And he had to more or less bring up the other children because of his own father's illness. There was never enough money, and his family lived with the uncertainty of not knowing whether they could afford the rent that month or if there would be food on the table.

"That sense of uncertainty is difficult for a young boy, and when your father reached manhood, he also reached for certainty. He worked hard, became a manager, left his roots behind, and through this he built a world where he felt secure. Do you think it is any accident that he chose a job in *life insurance*?

"There is a theme running through your father's life, as there is for all of us. Your father's theme is security versus insecurity, 'insurance' versus uncertainty, and it has played itself out through his work and his determination to bring order to his world. So I would say that your father's purpose is to explore this aspect of himself, and that the gift he brings to others is to offer them the same peace and comfort that he finds in order. He would regard this as the most profound blessing he can give them, even if he is 'only selling insurance.' That is his act of love and the way he plays out his purpose.

"Some people, however, confuse the power of love with the love of power. Your father could, for example, have chosen to sell people snake oil—or anything!—as a way of bringing security to himself. That would have been a way of playing out his purpose as well, but it would not be a healthy way for his soul or theirs, because love would not have been served. Your father's choice was to do the little things: to benefit others in terms he understood, and in this way he created a web of dreams for them, too."

Adam's words were touching and revealed a side to my father that I'd never seen before, where even selling insurance could be an act of love and frailty when looked at in a particular way. But I still found it difficult to reconcile day-to-day business with the business of saving souls. Adam, however, already had an answer prepared.

"Another way of looking at the nature of the soul is to imagine that there are four orders of men. There are those who remember their soul purpose clearly and act upon it. Let's call them the

Order of Priests and Healers, because their job is to bring love and peace to the world as the first and only truth.

"Then there are those who only vaguely remember their purpose and are fortunate that they act upon it in a way that does no harm. Most human beings are in this group—your father included. They engage with life—neither saints nor sinners— creating little acts of integrity and kindness from which others can learn and benefit. No matter how tiny or peripheral they seem to the lives of others, these acts of kindness are remembered in some small way because they are the actions of someone looking out for their fellow man and giving them a little help along the way. Let's call these people the Order of the Fortunate because, by accident or design, they do good in the world and live more or less sin-free lives, even if they are not really aware that they are fulfilling a mission at all. Or, at least, they do no harm.

"Then there are those who only vaguely remember their purpose, and in this they are not so different from the Fortunates, but they manage, through the life challenges they face and their inability to deal with them, to skew things away from love and into the realms of darkness. Let's call them the Order of the Damned.

"In recent history—less than thirty years, or a single generation ago, in fact—we have seen the actions of the Damned in the work of the great dictator Adolf Hitler. Hitler's soul mission may not have been so different from your father's or from most men's, believe it or not: he wanted to create order and security in the world as a result of his own childhood battles, but his answer was a New *World* Order where he alone could feel safe. By turning his love inwards, he forgot the most important reason for our being here: *to love others*. In so doing, he created a web of lies and suffering, not dreams: the very opposite of his soul's greater purpose.

"Hitler and others like him—tyrants, bullies, and those lost in ego, as much as world dictators—are the closest we know to evil. They are sinners because they go against the real order of the universe—and for that we should have compassion. There, by the grace of God, we do not have to tread, because we can learn from their mistakes instead of sharing their illusions and pain.

"And finally, there are those who never wake up and remember their reason for being. They bumble through life not knowing what they're doing from one moment to the next, seekers without purpose, bees without hives, flowers without sunlight. Whatever they randomly create they also destroy at random, and then re-create it again, endlessly, over and over, because they have no clear direction in life. Those who seek love but cannot give it, those who seek power but cannot handle the power that others give them, those who look for purpose in a million different places but cannot settle on any one: the world is full of such people. Let's call them the Order of Fools, because they are always busy doing nothing and getting nothing done!

"In these four orders, most of life and our journeys on Earth are represented. Amongst us we have people who know their soul's purpose and act upon it; people who are never fully aware of their purpose but manage, nonetheless, to do good and achieve at least part of their mission regardless; those who never become aware of their purpose and manage to do only harm; and those who are unaware that they have a purpose and who, through their confusion, achieve nothing of any value, good or evil; it is as if they were never here.

"There is hope for the first two orders—the Priests and the Fortunates—and, although it is a struggle, *some* hope for the souls of the others. Alongside the cloud of awareness, however, to which our souls will one day return, there is a web of despair for the orders of the Damned and the Fools. Some, I suppose, call it purgatory. It is a 'cooling off' place for those who've wasted their time on Earth or who realize in death that they have done harm in life through their confusion and lack of awareness. They remain in that web until their souls return to wholeness. Only then can they rejoin their community, after they are 'decontaminated,' as it were."

I felt a shock of recognition at Adam's words. His description of the "cloud of awareness" and the "web of despair" was so close to what I had seen during my vision in the oak that I shuddered inwardly at the memory of those grey, lifeless faces. I wanted to know if this was a literal truth or a metaphor. Had I seen something "real" or had I received a more spiritual truth, from which my mind had created a picture?

Once again, Adam's answer was cryptic. "Of course I am speaking in symbols, because symbols are the language the soul understands. But this does not make them any less true. Symbols, after all, are what this world is made from. What is a rose, or a flag, or a Catholic mass, or a government? They are real in themselves and yet they are also symbols so strong that some people choose to live, love, and die by them. So, yes, I am speaking in metaphor, and no doubt you saw a metaphor for the truth as well, but it was also the absolute truth.

"There is a web of dreams and a web of lies that we can give our energy to. One will take us home and one will leave us hanging. So, you see, to be truly alive in this world—to do no harm and to fulfill your soul's purpose so you move closer to love—you have to know what that purpose is."

Adam's views on sin, right-living, and the four orders of man was either mystifying or enlightening—I couldn't decide which. Either way, it seemed radical and nothing like the versions I had heard in religious lessons, where people were either "good" or "bad" and destined for "Heaven" or "Hell" because of their deeds on Earth. In Adam's system of belief, even Hitler—an easy target for a vengeful world or a Christian god, and a prime candidate, I would have thought, for everlasting fire—was "the closest we know to evil," and not, I presumed from this, evil per se.

"Our first—and, fundamentally, our *only*—purpose is to love," Adam explained again. "The ranting god of our Old Testament makes for an interesting read but must have been misguided—or, more likely, misquoted—to insist on evil as a natural state. If we are all made perfect in God's image, after all, then what does the existence of evil and 'original sin' say about him? It is best to remember that Bibles are written by men, not by the gods, and in reading them, you should choose your passages carefully!

"I have worked with 'sin' all my life, and it is apparent to me that there is no such thing as evil. There is only misguided love.

"In this world, we learn how to love from our parents and, as children, our experience of life is so small that we have no one else to ask, nor the words or means by which to frame a question. Imagine, then, if you had been brought up in a home where your mother was emotionally scarred, abusive, a bully and a liar, or who doted on you and treated you as her possession; that would be your only experience of how love is given and, most likely, that is how you would grow to love as well. This, incidentally, is something like Hitler's upbringing, but it is by no means unique.

"Children brought up in such a way come to realize two things: that they are the most important things in the world, and their egos are fed from this; but also that love can be taken from them and is therefore a means of punishment and control. In all innocence, they absorb this knowledge and it comes to inform their souls.

"In trying to give love they follow what they have learned, and the outcome is not 'evil' but a misguided attempt at love. They may cause harm to others through these attempts, but they are also in pain. They look around them and see that their way of love is unwanted and unwholesome in its effects, and that they themselves are undesirable. Time and again they are rejected, but still they know no other way.

"These adult children are sinners, not because they are inherently evil, but because they have never challenged love to discover its truths for themselves or explored the wisdom of their souls. And yet all they need do is remember, because, as the Bible tells us, in each of us 'dwelleth all the fullness of the Godhead bodily'.[8] I am, of course, choosing my passages carefully! We are gods, in other words, and our souls hold our answers of what is right and wrong. But to realize that we have to know our souls."

---

8   The reference here is from Colossians 2:9.

Shadows had climbed the walls and were licking at the ceiling as we sat before the fire in Adam's cottage. He rose and went into the kitchen, returning with a glass of amber liquid for us both. "Meddyglyn," he said.

Meddyglyn is, from the Welsh, "medicinal liquor": warm mead made from fermented honey, water, and yeast, blended with herbs and spices—in this case, it seemed to me, now that my tastebuds were becoming attuned to the plant teas that Adam often prepared for us, a mix of chamomile and lavender.

"You have a question," he said as he sat down again and placed his glass at his side. "Perhaps the most important question of all."

"If what you say is true," I replied, "I suppose it is the most important thing I could ask: how do we know what our soul purpose is?"

"It is different for everyone," he said. "But that's not what you're really asking, is it? What you want to know is 'How do *I* find *my* soul purpose?' You must be more precise with your questions if you insist on asking them! But, in fact, the answer is simple: meaning is revealed in the meaningless.

"In other words: whatever we do—even the things we do seemingly at random; perhaps especially those things—can show us the deeper truths of our souls. The abstract, ambiguous, or absurd carry our meanings just as much as the things we carefully plan and commit to.

"Two people may look at a tree or a star, for example—one a poet, the other a scientist. One sees a collection of gasses or chemical processes, the other sees a poem. Neither is correct and neither can say that they know what a tree or a star really is, because neither of them has experienced the world as the thing they observe. And yet each will find meaning in his own way by seeing himself in the thing he relates to. If you want to know what your soul's purpose is, therefore, look at the meanings you give things and at the patterns that run through your life.

"Nature is our greatest teacher in this, as it is with all things," he continued, as we stepped out into the garden. "So, I am going to leave you alone with nature and, since everything we do has meaning, there are no instructions. Do as you wish between now and the time I come for you. Explore the garden and look for your meanings. Just hold in mind your intention to know your soul."

The garden was twilight and shadows, the night air balmy, and I entered it without a clue what to do next.

At the end of Adam's garden was a stream—really a ditch which caught the water that ran off from the fields and was always of varying depth. It claimed my attention, so I chose to sit by that. This time of year it was half-filled, and as the moonlight caught its ripples, it became full of silver threads.

I did what I had been taught: I slowed down, breathed deeply, and let my eyes go out of focus as I gazed at the patterns that moonlight makes on water. Silence enveloped me, apart from the night breeze in the leaves and the distant bark of a dog.

After a time—who can say how long when there is no time to measure by?—the water started to change. Moonlight became an artist's brush and the ripples the moon's creation. I saw what at first seemed a random procession of images but which, on closer inspection, appeared to have a strange order and symmetry to them, like some weird evolution playing out on the ripples: sparks, planets, reptiles, trees, a ridiculous dog spinning and chasing its own tail, serpents coiling and uncoiling, stooping humanoids learning to stand, a footprint in moon dust; the entire procession repeating over and over. Its cycles seemed packed with meaning, as if, by deciphering the water's code, I could understand the entire history and future of humankind and, at the same time, I knew that it was all mundane and meaningless, and I was just a boy staring down at a puddle. I understood exactly what Adam had meant: that I was dreaming it all and giving meaning where there was intrinsically none.

There was more to it than that, though. It was as if the world responded to me as I made sense of its clues, so that each image was not just a picture but a feeling it left with me. In this way, the world and I fashioned each other, and there was no separation between us. I was a part of this strange evolution myself.

At some point I realized that Adam was standing beside me. "What do you see?" he asked.

"Images repeating," I answered.

"And what do they *mean* to you? How do you *feel* when you see them?"

"Reassured; as if there is a sense to it all and that the world will always be here. Confused, too; unsure of whether the world is creating me or I'm creating it: as if I'm a part of it but looking in on it, and at the same time, as if it couldn't exist without me. Everything is full of meaning and yet means nothing."

Adam listened quietly and then, after a respectful silence, said, "Unfortunate." I felt a jolt at the word.

"You wanted to know your soul's purpose," he said, "and I stand to be corrected because the truth of one who is living it is always more important than that of a bystander, but it seems to me that you are lost in wonder. You are amazed at the world and its spirit, and your mission, therefore, is to reveal its beauty to others.

"I say it is unfortunate because most people have lost their sense of wonder at the beauty that surrounds them and will resist it at every turn when they are reminded of the truth: that the world, for all its sadness, is still a place of majesty and one which is worthy of love, not the suffering we inflict on it or on each other.

"If they feel a stirring in their souls at all, they will put it down to imagination or to the moment and soon forget it. Or, worse still, they will believe that you created this feeling in them through some act of poetry, magic, or 'witchcraft,' not because they have seen the face of God in the trees and streams.

"All of this means that you will stand outside the world of men and have to create your own web of dreams. This is always the loneliest way, and sometimes the saddest, when, from this perspective, we more clearly see the world and the sorrows that people carry.

"To stand outside is the course I chose, too, but I used it to my advantage by becoming a healer for others. Perhaps that is ultimately your path, too, but unlike me, you have not made your choices yet, and so for now you are truly alone."

5

The Sins of the Serpent-Filled Woman

> Behold Adam is become as one of us,
> knowing good and evil ...
>
> *Genesis 2: 22*

ADAM DILWYN VAUGHAN knew good and evil. In his tradition, a sin was a blemish or a weight on the soul which held it trapped in a sort of perdition or limbo—a web of lies—while that sin remained. His job was to free the soul by devouring that blemish.

But it was not just the souls of the dead that the sin eater cared for. The living, too—perhaps more especially the living—carry the weight of sin, which they may also continue to accumulate or lose their power to in a way that the dead cannot because the living are, by definition, alive and still at risk. Their aliveness also gives them the opportunity to release their sins, however, and to find redemption by bringing their souls back to balance.

I had been visiting Adam for a few years now, following no set schedule, and I had never arrived at his cottage to find anyone else there. Until today.

Having knocked at his door, I was quite used to letting myself in if Adam was not in his garden, which is where I most often found him. Walking into his front room this time, however, I was met with the sight of him and an old woman I recognized from the village. My shock at this was not just in seeing Adam with someone else but that the woman was one of those who, some years ago, had warned me away from his cottage.

"A place of strange lights," she had called it. I had never known what she meant by that, but now, as I looked in at them both, there did seem a strange, smoky light to the room, along with the pungent aroma of rosemary.

Both of them looked up as I entered. The woman seemed horrified to see me and crossed herself, muttering beneath her breath, but Adam just smiled. "Could you wait outside for a moment," he said. "I'll be out."

I backed away, closing the door behind me, and waited for Adam to join me in the garden, which he did a few minutes later, laughing quietly to himself, but with such an intensity that he was almost bent double.

"You gave her quite a start!" he said through his laughter. "You know her from the village, of course, but I imagine you had no idea she was a patient of mine—has been for the last ten years, but she'll never talk about it with others. It wouldn't be in her interests in a community like ours.

"She comes to me when she needs healing, and now that her secret's out, she's given permission for you to come in and watch if you want.

"I told her you were my sorcerer's apprentice," he chuckled, "so you'll probably have some questions to answer when you get home! Just sit quietly when you come in, and observe. If you have any questions—and, knowing you, there will be hundreds!—I'll answer them later, agreed?"

I re-entered the smoky light and sat quietly, as I had been told. The old lady hadn't moved and sat upright on a hard-backed wooden chair with her hands folded in her lap and her eyes closed. Adam resumed his position standing behind her and closed his eyes as well. A stillness entered the room.

Looking around, I noticed a rough stone bowl beneath the old lady's chair from which the smoke of burning rosemary arose, wrapping itself in silent fronds around the self-professed sorcerer and his patient.

Adam's eyes opened slightly, following the smoke as it drifted around her. From time to time, he would use his hands to push it further in towards her or to brush it away from her body. Once in a while he would also grab at the smoke, as if wrestling with something more tangible, then take it to his mouth and swallow, as if eating or drinking it in, sometimes coughing like he was fighting an instinct to retch.

After a little while of watching this, my eyes began to play tricks on me, as it seemed, in the still air of the room, that there really *was* something more tangible to the smoke. I allowed myself to slow down, to breathe deeply, and for my eyes to relax their focus. And then I saw it.

What Adam was holding was not smoke at all but strings of slime, grey-black or flecked with bile-green and yellow, and with the consistency of snot. I gasped, causing Adam to glance at me, and wondered how I had not seen it before. How could I have mistaken these threads for smoke?

Some of them changed form as he held them and became worms or snakes writhing in his hands and trying to wriggle free as he closed his mouth around them. Some were larger, darker, and looked to me as if they knew exactly what was happening. They had mouths of their own and sharp teeth with which they snapped at his face. Adam's response was swift: holding them with one hand, he used his other to break their necks so that they, too, could be devoured. As I grew more accustomed to the room and the sight before me, I thought with disgust that I could hear the snaps of their necks, their wails, snarls, and curses.

After some minutes of this, the room took on another change as the threads became smoke again, with nothing more repellent within it. Adam stepped away from the woman and picked up a bundle of leaves. He began to brush her with this and to shake it around her so that a hissing, rattling sound filled the air as he traced a route from her head to her feet on either side of her body and all around her. As he reached her feet he made a scooping or brushing movement, as if pulling something from her, and then used the leaves to flick it out through the window to my right.

He chanted, almost under his breath, as he completed these maneuvers.

To the willows, to the oak, to the clouds,
To the flowers of the fields and hedgerows,
To the stream, to the dark hills beyond,
To the caves and holy wells.

Then, without a backward glance, he cast the leaves away into the hearth behind him, where the fire ate them up. For a second more, I thought I heard snarls and moans as the flames devoured the leaves and the shadows of the hearth became serpents writhing and spitting fire as they dissipated into smoke.

Adam was standing in silence behind his patient now as if in prayer, his hands resting lightly on the crown of her head. Slowly he removed one hand and raised it into the air. He snapped his fingers three times and whistled. "I call the angels of the storms to blow through this woman and bless her," he said quietly, and then:

Peace of the singing summer breeze be upon you
Power of the dreaming hills
Wisdom of the hawk and the endurance of mountains
Grace of the protective wings and whispered breath of angels.

Each time before he spoke he raised his hand again as if to receive these blessings and then gently returned it to the woman's head as if bestowing them upon her, blowing softly through her hair with each boon bestowed as if his breath would disperse these gifts throughout her soul.

I call the angels of the storms to purify,
cleanse, and protect this woman
And to blow away entanglements of darkness.

I noticed that the wind blew a little more strongly in the garden, rustling the leaves of the trees. A bird began to sing, the sheep in the distance began their braying chatter, and the stream spoke up with gurgling voice, where before there had been silence. At last, he spoke again:

We thank you for your mercy and healing
We release you now so you may serve others
as you have served us here
In the name of the Father, Son, and Holy Spirit,
I set you free. Caritas.[9]

The smoke no longer rose from the bowl beneath the chair, and the room became, once more, simply a room.

"We are done for today," said Adam, and the old lady stood up. "Try to keep yourself clean until we meet again—which I hope will not be for a while!" Then he handed her a bottle containing

---

9   Latin: "love and wisdom."

a mixture of herbs, with the words: "This will help you. Drink from it three times a day until it is empty, just to be sure."

The woman smiled her thanks and, nodding only to me, eyes to the ground, left the cottage.

"I am sure you have plenty of questions," said Adam. "But there are a few things I need to do first, so can you wait a moment?"

For once, however, I had no questions—or, rather, so many that I didn't know where to begin. I was sitting, mouth open, I'm sure, in stunned silence, and could manage only: "What do you need to do?"

"Oh, that," said Adam. "I need to vomit."

HE WALKED OUT into the garden and towards the plants that grew there, me following behind, still unsure of what to make of the events I had seen or how I should act now. Adam knelt before one of the plants and dug a shallow hole in the soil with his hands, then reached into his pocket and brought out a handful of salt, which he put to his lips and ate.

Bending forwards, he began to retch into the hole. The flowers above him seemed almost to shudder and pull back. Nothing solid emerged from his mouth, however: only the air of his lungs. The dry retching continued for a little while, then he covered over the soil and stood up.

He said nothing but beckoned me to follow as he went back into the house and straight to the kitchen. I sat down in the front room and waited until he returned, bringing two cups with him. "Dandelion root," he said. "Roasted, with warm milk. Nothing better as a pick-you-up!"

I still said nothing. I was coming to terms with the strangeness of what I had witnessed, and I was still young enough not to make judgements, but an unusual mood had come over me. I felt, I suppose, a little abandoned, if that is the correct word.

In all the time I had known Adam, he had never shown me this side of himself. I knew, of course, that he had been a sin eater as a younger man in Wales, and I knew that he had knowledge of plants and herbs from what he had shown and told me, but to see him healing someone, especially when I had drawn the conclusion—wrongly, it seemed—that he had retired from his profession, left me feeling that there were deeper secrets that I had been excluded from.

He had anticipated my mood. "Do you know why sin eaters live on the edges of villages and not at their hearts?" he asked. I shook my head. "Because we are kings and lepers.

"We are kings because we are central to the community we serve. No one who has sinned can enter Heaven without us because the weight on their soul is too great.

"But we are still lepers because we are unclean: we take the sins of others upon ourselves, as you saw me doing today, and we free the sinners from shame."

He paused and sipped his tea. "If you think about that for a moment, there is a paradox in what I just said, because if I am unclean, it is because of the sins of *others*. I am pure until the moment I see a patient because only by being pure can I absorb their sin—if I am too full of my own sins, there is no room for theirs—and I am pure the moment afterwards because I know how to release those sins again, as you watched me do in the garden.

"The reason that sin eaters live at the edge, then, is that the community is afraid to look at itself and see its own sins revealed. I am a reminder of forces in the world and in their souls that they do not care to see. But I am also their salvation. Curious, is it not?

"There is an expression in Wales: *Fo byd ben byd bont*—'Who would be a leader must first be a bridge.' While I have no desire to be a leader, I am a bridge for the people I serve: a bridge between this world and the next, between their failings and their possibility of perfection, between the light and the shade. And so I keep their secrets, as I should and must. They know they can come to me and be helped and that no one—before you today—will know of their visit. That is why I have not told you of my work. But now that you know, I will, of course, help you make sense of it.

"Chance brought you here today, and chance—or the will of God—is *why* you were brought. It has never been *my* will to teach or tell you anything, only to be available in case chance should bring you to my door, which it has done many times now."

In later years, I would come to understand that solitariness is a condition among most people of spiritual power. A time of aloneness is a requisite in many of the shamanic initiations I have subsequently undertaken, and in several traditions the shaman must also live on the outskirts of his community because his power is too great and what he represents is too dangerous for him to be at its center. The aloneness of the shaman stands, in a physical and symbolic way, for his dwelling on the thresholds of reality, the betwixt-and-between places of human and spirit connection.

In our fairy tales and myths, witches, wizards, and other gifted madmen always live alone and in shadowlands, too, like Merlin, the shaman-healer of King Arthur, who for seven years remained alone in the forests, learning from nature during his upward descent into madness and the brilliance of his dark enlightenment.

Shamans know that human beings—and, indeed, all things—are energy or spirit rather than physical form. It is this energy, in fact, which gives rise to form and is the healing currency of the shaman.

Energy is, in the sin eater's terms, the natural spirit or potential we are born with, from which we grow our souls, and later it is the soul itself. Shamans in all cultures—whether they are sin eaters or not, and whatever their views on the nature and origin of the soul—believe that this energy can be corrupted in three ways.

Firstly, it can become blocked or dissipated, so we are no longer in touch with our souls. This happens every day in the modern world, where we are required to work at an unnatural pace and to put the needs of others before our own. We forget how to nurture our souls and we spread ourselves too thinly. This is what our energy does, too: spreads itself so thinly that we become weak and no longer in touch with our power.

When this happens, like a battery drawn from too often, we become run-down. Our energy becomes permeable, and without a solid boundary of protection, illness of a physical, mental, emotional, or spiritual nature can arise. This is the situation, for example, that front-line troops had found themselves in during the Second World War, which, at the time I first knew Adam, had only ended thirty years before and whose dark memories the sin eater dealt with, from time to time, in the patients he saw.

Under continual bombardment, unable to rest, and conditioned to think of the country's "victory" more than of personal survival, it became a medical fact that young soldiers would inevitably experience "shell shock" (today we would say "post-traumatic stress disorder") within just thirty days of deployment to a front-line position. Hence the need for a continual stream of fresh blood as thousands of young men became spiritually sick and emotionally and mentally destroyed. It was not death or physical injury that laid waste to these men but trauma that consumed them.

Secondly, in shamanism there is a notion of "soul loss." This is when circumstances around us or in which we are involved become so horrific that parts of our energy splinter off so we are no longer fully present.

For their own protection, these parts of the soul go into hiding, carrying our feelings and awareness with them. Then we cannot know or live our soul's purpose because the soul is no longer whole or available for us to draw from, but at least we are safe from the corruption and horror—the lack of love—around us.

This, again, might be the case for a soldier surrounded by death: constantly alert to the possibility of being killed, watching his friends die around him, and, perhaps more damaging still, being forced to kill others against his awareness—no matter how slight—of the true purpose of his soul: to love, create, and bring life.

It is also the situation of a child abused by a parent, a woman or man suffering an unhappy marriage and trapped by circumstances they must endure, or that of a lover who has given her heart so deeply that it feels like it was ripped from her chest on the day her beloved left her.

In each case, the power of that child, man, or woman is lost to them and they become wraiths: those who wander through life sad, distressed, confused, or simply "not there," awaiting the return of their souls so they can reconnect with their purpose and rekindle their joy in living. That soul part may never return, however, while the abuse or the pain continues. Without the help of a shaman they might never find themselves again and may go through life as people not fully alive.

The third way that the soul may be corrupted is through what shamans call "spirit intrusions." This is where somebody else's energy comes to infect our souls. In rare cases this arises through deliberate acts of sorcery, where a "spiritual virus" is intentionally sent to attack a rival and feed off that person's energy like a parasite, leaving them depleted, open to illness, and—if the intrusion is not removed—available to death.

It is unnecessary for the attack to be deliberate, however, and more frequently spirit intrusions are not acts of terror but acts of error or, in Adam's words, acts of "misguided love." In a world of competition, conflict, and despair, anger and frustration directed towards others have become the norm as we have lost sight of our souls. We increasingly have come to believe in a world of scarcity, where we are in competition with others and wish them to have less so that we may have more of what we believe, in our illusion, to be the limited resources available. And so we send prayers for our ascension and the decline and fall of others almost as our daily practice, and in this way our prayers become curses. And yet it is our own souls that suffer. "A bad tree bears bad fruit" (Matthew 7:17), just as a sick society creates its own sickness.

There is a parallel here with the Buddhist notion of right-living: that no matter what others do to us, there is a correct way for us to behave in order to preserve our spiritual integrity and the purpose of our souls. Even if we do not understand right from wrong in a world where ethics are fluid, our souls know the truth, and so we may carry guilt and shame within us, gnawing away at our spirits or waiting like a time bomb to explode when the weight of our sins finally becomes unbearable. It is this we must try to avoid by divesting our souls of sin and making a commitment to right-living now.

We can also feel the corrosive effects of sin by being in the presence of the wrongdoings of others. It is not necessary for us to sin, only to tolerate the sinner, because then their sins become ours.

This concept is not as simple as it seems, however. It means, for example, that even if we have been sinned *against* and are victims, the guilt and shame of others can become our cross to bear. The victim of abuse, for example, may sometimes feel, at an unconscious level, that they were somehow to blame or that they "invited" such abuse. This may or may not be true, but it is the *belief* itself rather than what happened that may cause the wound to the soul. By holding on to the event, that is, and thereby "tolerating the presence of the sinner," we can damage ourselves. Removing ourselves from the presence of sin therefore means letting go, forgiving the sinner and ourselves, and releasing the attachments we feel to the sinful event instead of allowing it to define us, for none of us are truly victims unless we choose that for ourselves.

For the sin eater, all of these routes to illness eventually become one because the first, only, and original sin is subscribing to illusion.

In Adam's view, human beings are born perfect. Having just arrived in the Garden from the world of spirit or "God"—the great cloud of loving awareness from which all things are born— it could not be any other way, since we carry perfection within us. Thus, choosing our passages carefully, we read in Genesis 6:2 that, in our Garden of perfection, we are all the "sons of God."

Two trees grow in this Garden: the Tree of Life and the Tree of the Knowledge of Good and Evil. In Adam's interpretation of what happened next, God forbade us to eat from the Tree of Knowledge, warning us that we would die if we did. In other words, that we would lose our connection to our original state of bliss and become aware of our separation and individuality. Conflict and suffering would arise from this, which would create the forms of dis-ease that shamans know and heal.

When man, regardless, ate from the tree, the world of illusion was born. It is illusion because, underlying all of the apparently separate forms that then appeared, we all remain one, connected by our souls to the cloud of divine energy we were born from. Our first sin—the original sin of the Bible—is therefore to lose sight of our origins (hence, *original* sin) and to forget the purpose of our souls in having made our journeys to Earth, which is to know, to explore, and to experience. All of these things are only possible in a world of separate forms, but irrespective of this and crucially, we must maintain our connection to *love*.

Man was not forbidden to eat from the Tree of Life, however, and indeed was given permission to do so. Thus, in Genesis 3:22 we read the words of God that man "has become like one of Us, knowing good and evil; and now he might stretch out his hand and take also from the tree of life, and eat, and live forever."

Adam had two comments to make on this Bible passage. The first is that, evidently, there is more than one god. The "one of Us" who speaks in Genesis Adam equated with all of the souls contained within the great community that is the cloud of awareness, where there is individual consciousness together with a unity of loving purpose. From this perspective, the words of "God" in Genesis are rather like a stage aside, one "God" to another, and not judgemental, but more of an update on what is happening on Earth: "Our alchemy is working, God is becoming human, spirit is becoming matter, so that we may experience the world."

Adam's other observation was that by eating from the Tree of Knowledge and thereby honoring God's true purpose, man is able to bring love and perfection to the Garden through his life and actions. It is because of this that man might "live forever" and make a "Heaven on Earth," extending the cloud of awareness and contributing to the spiritual evolution of the universe as a whole. It was not only inevitable, therefore, but *desirous and intended* that man should seek knowledge, because only in this is God's purpose served.

In a sense, then, man is a pioneer, a colonizer of worlds, his soul-essence voyaging out beyond the cloud to create entire new worlds of love. His *origin*al sin, and the cause of his suffering, was simply to forget this great soul-mission and become lost in his purposeful creation: the world of illusions and forms.

Looked at in this way, the work of the sin eater and shaman is simply to help people remember—literally, to re-member: to come back together—to rediscover our purpose and to recover the bliss that we have forgotten so that our souls become whole and healed once again.

Thus, the three causes of illness or "sin"—energy imbalance, soul loss, and spirit intrusion—all arise from *origin*al sin: our belief in separation. For, after all, how can energy leak away from us or become corrupt if there is only one energy in the world, which is perfect and shared by us all? How can we lose soul when we are all *one soul* and part of all-that-is? How can anyone's energy intrude upon ours when we are all *the same* energy?

These are the mysteries of the world, and all of us must ask and answer these questions for ourselves as we take our journeys back to perfection.

6

The Nature of Healing

> ❧ O God! Can I not save
> One from the pitiless wave?
> Is all that we see or seem
> But a dream within a dream?
>
> *Edgar Allan Poe,*
> *"A Dream Within a Dream"*

"No healing can be fully explained in words," Adam told me. "The realizations of the soul do not and cannot come from logic and formal explanation; they arise from subtle understandings that call us back to our purpose, our faith, to love and the truth of the heart. This call is heard through song, poetry, and fable, and through the rituals of healing themselves.

"It is for this reason that I am going to tell you a story. It is a tale of faith, courage, and love that can overcome even the death of the soul.

"In the customs of Wales, it is a tradition to watch over a corpse for three nights after death. This is the story of one such corpse-watcher, a maiden called Sheen, who was named, I suppose, for the brightness of her faith and the gold of her heart. Close your eyes and put thinking out of your mind so you may listen with *your* heart."

The Heart So True: A Unique Tale

A neighbor came to Sheen's door one evening when it was neither light nor dark. Sheen opened the house to her, for she knew that something was to be told.

The Hunter-King had been found dead in the woods, the neighbor woman said, and he was being waked in her house. Her eldest daughter had been the corpse-watcher the first night, praying for him and watching over his body lest his soul should wander. In the morning, the girl's hand was found withered and burned, and she was white with fear.

The woman's second daughter had been the watcher on the next night, and her hand had been left trembling as if with cold. Now it was the third and last night of the wake, and there was no one to watch the corpse.

Sheen had been sweet on the Hunter-King, and now that he was dead she felt that nothing good could ever happen in the world. "Will you watch, and I will give you a comb for your hair?" asked her neighbor. Sheen thought, sadly, that there was no aloneness so great as that of a corpse with no one to watch it on its last strange night above ground, and, saying she would watch, she made her way to the wake-house.

At first, she was afraid to look at the bed where the body lay. Then at last she went over and saw the Hunter-King with his still-handsome face, coins upon his eyes, and the plate of salt upon his chest. With a tear, she lit candles and placed them in the windows. Then she began her watching.

Late into the night, Sheen began to search for more candles so that she might be able to light new ones as the others went out. But as she rose, all of the candles blew out at once, and in the darkness a moaning filled the air. Then, by the light of the window and the moon that shone through it, she saw the corpse of the Hunter-King sit up on the bed where it had lain.

Something in Sheen overcame her dread, and she went over to the corpse and took the salt from its breast and put it on her lips and its own. When that was done, the corpse began to speak.

"Fair maid," it said, "have you the courage to follow me? The daughters of this house have failed and they have been stricken. But have you a true heart and are you faithful?"

"I do, and I will follow you," said Sheen.

"Then," said the corpse, "put your hands on my shoulders. We must cross the Quaking Bog, and the Burning Forest, and then the Icy Sea." Sheen put her hands on the shoulders of the Hunter-King, and a great storm came. Together they were swept through the roof of the house and into the soul of the night.

After much travelling, down they came to the ground, and the dead man sprang away from Sheen. She went to follow him and found her feet upon the Quaking Bog. The corpse of the Hunter-King went ahead, and she knew that she must keep it in sight.

He moved so swiftly that Sheen could almost not keep pace, and then the earth went from beneath her feet and she fell into the watery mud. She struggled out and then jumped another pool that was hidden with heather, all the time in dread that she would lose sight of the figure before her. She sank and struggled and sprang across swamp and morass, and all the time the corpse of the Hunter-King went ahead.

Then she saw fires against the night and knew that they were approaching the Burning Forest. The figure before her sprang across a ditch and into the trees. Sheen sprang across it, too, as burning branches fell across her path and hot winds burned her face. The bright flames dazzled her and the smoke made her weep, but the figure before her went on, and Sheen went on, too.

The forest ended at a perilous cliff. Below was the Icy Sea. The corpse of the Hunter-King dived, and Sheen followed. The cold water chilled her marrow, and she thought the ice would drive the life from her. But the corpse swam before her, so she swam on.

And then they were on land again. "Fair maid," said the corpse of the Hunter-King, "put your hands on my shoulders." She did so and the mighty storm came again and swept them both away. They were driven once again through the roof of the neighbor woman's house. The candlewicks fluttered in the wake-room and sprang to life again. She saw the corpse where it laid, and its eyes were open now.

"Fair maid," said the Hunter-King, "you have brought me back to life. I was a man under enchantment. There is a witch in the woods whom I once loved before I fell out of love with her. She enchanted me so that my soul was out of my body and wandering away, and I could not love another. It was my lost soul that you followed.

"The enchantment I was under could only be broken when I found a heart so true that its owner would follow me over Quaking Bog, through Burning Forest, and across Icy Sea only for the good of my soul. You have brought me back to life."

He took her hands then and they were warm in hers. Sheen felt a joy like no other as he sang of his love for her, of the brightness of her hair and the blue of her eyes.

"Fair maid," he said, "is there anything that binds you to this place?" There was not, and so "Come with me to my kingdom," said the Hunter-King, "and you shall be my wife and the love of my heart." The Hunter-King lifted her before him onto the back of his stallion, and they rode into his kingdom.[10]

◆ ◆ ◆

"So you see," said Adam, "there are enchantments in the world: energies, curses, and attachments that can take our life-force from us and leave our souls lost in a place of illusion. But these enchantments can also be broken and our souls made whole through an act of love and healing faith.

"It was nature itself and the elements—the wind, the earth, the fire, and the water—that restored the soul, and the healer—Sheen—who acted as the guide. She did so because her heart was true, and she was not lost in the realms of illusion but understood that love and wonder are the most important powers on Earth. This understanding can only be found in nature, but, once found, it will bring us home to love through the rediscovery of our souls and their purpose.

"The woman you saw me healing is a nurse," said Adam, breaking his muse. "She works amongst the sick and dying—a corpse-watcher of sorts, you might say. Inevitably, her faith is tested and she absorbs many energies from her patients, and from the doctors and nurses too, all of whom work in a place of suffering.

---

10 The story of Sheen, the corpse-watcher, is extracted and adapted from *The King of Ireland's Son* by Padraic Colum (1916). The text is available at http://ftp .fortunaty.net/text/sacred-texts/neu/celt/kis/kis36.htm, current as of April 5, 2008.

"What you saw me doing was removing those attachments so she could recover and, in her quiet moments of restored balance and greater fortitude, remember what she came here to do. Her 'sin,' if we wish to call it that, was forgetting; the spirits within her were the consequence."

I told Adam what I had seen during the healing and asked him to explain, from his point of view, what had happened.

"Insofar as any healing can be explained in words, the smoke that you saw is a 'doctor,' a purifier which also carries our prayers for healing. It will show you, as it clings to the body or is repelled, where that person lacks energy or is carrying the spirit of others. Once this is revealed, we can remove those energies so her own spirit can flow and her soul come back into balance."

It sounded innocent and obvious as Adam spoke, but to me these energies had appeared as repulsive worms, serpents, and leeches. I asked Adam what he had seen.

"Oh, something very similar!" he laughed. "Do not be confused, though. The fact that we see them like that does not mean that is their true form. Remember that energy is simply energy, and all of it is part of one soul. The reason you and I see energy in this way is so it is clear to us. By its repugnance we know it is something that does not naturally belong in that person's body and then it can be removed. But do not judge it as having no value or beauty of its own."

"Some of the energy I saw seemed to be fighting you. It had teeth."

"Of course. All spirit is alive. It has its purpose, too, suffers its own illusions and has its own will to live. It is trying only to survive, and so, to it, I am the aggressor.

"Let us not delude ourselves. I am a murderer when I take that spirit out, just as a doctor who removes a cancer is also a murderer, because, in the whole scheme of things, even the spirit of a cancer has a right to live—as does the patient. Both are alive, aware, and have hopes for their own evolution; it is only our human judgments that make one worth saving and the other not.

"For the sin that I commit by healing, I must make my confession and prayers for forgiveness, and perhaps the doctor may make his, but we cannot be anything other than what we are. It is our purpose to heal, and we can only hope that we have made the right choices and that, on balance, we add to the good of the world."

In subsequent years, I have seen many shamanic extractions—the removal of energies that are of no use to the person who comes for healing—and they take many forms. Some shamans suck the energy from the body, some grab it with their hands as Adam had done, some—in the Amazon—use a bundle of leaves similar to those that Adam had also used, which they call a *chapaca*. The job of the chapaca, when rubbed down the body or shaken around the patient, is to absorb energies so they can be disposed of. I asked one of these shamans once how he had learned this healing approach. "Simple," he said. "The spirits taught me."[11]

It seems remarkable that shamans thousands of miles from each other who have never met or even heard of each other use similar healing approaches and tools, have the same understanding of illness, know how to defeat it, and have the same ethical concerns about doing so, but I have learned to accept what they tell me: that if we open our ears—and our hearts—spirit will teach us all we need to know.

A number of things within Adam's healing still intrigued me: the casting out of "sins" to "the willows, the oak, and the clouds," for example; the blessings Adam had brought back for his patient; the vomiting; and the herbs he had given his patient to take away.

"When an energy is removed, it must be broken up so it cannot reconstitute and do further harm," said Adam. "And so I give it to my allies in nature—the trees, the clouds, the plants, and so on. The spirit of each has agreed to work with me, to accept the

---

11 There is more information on shamanic healing, soul retrieval, extraction medicine, and the use of the chapaca in my book *Plant Spirit Shamanism: Traditional Techniques for Healing the Soul* (Destiny Books, 2006). For information on shamanic healing in general, see my book *The Journey to You: A Shaman's Path to Empowerment* (Bantam Books, 2001).

energies I give them, and to transform them, returning them to the earth so that they become pure again.

"No energy is truly 'good' or 'bad,' you see; those are just labels we apply to the things that serve or do not serve us as human beings. The energies in my patient were spirits which, to another person, might be exactly what they need, and so I release them in the hope that they find a compatible partner. In this way, these spirits find their purer form and, when drawn in by someone in need, can offer the healing required. Then the sufferer can recover and the spirits have a chance to evolve through love.

"In return for the help of my allies in nature, I feed and honor them. The oak that you sat in all those moons ago is one of my allies, for example, and you may have noticed ribbons tied to its branches to honor its spirit. Every plant or flower that I work with receives love and care, and there is not one in this garden that is not given the attention it needs to grow healthy and strong.

"It is the same with the blessings, all of them the gifts of the allies in spirit that it is my great good fortune to work with. You will notice that they are all natural spirits—the summer breeze, the hills, the raven, and the mountains—and all have gifts to impart: cleansing, endurance, wisdom, farsightedness—because nature is a living thing and every part of it has a restorative essence or quality, as we saw in the tale of the Hunter-King.

This is also the reason that we can read omens from nature and thereby take God's good advice. That is for another day, however, so we do not complicate things here.

"What you need to know in terms of this healing is that blessings of peace, power, and grace were returned to that woman, which were exactly what she needed to be strong and well."

"Are you saying, then, that the angels are also your allies?" I recalled Adam's final blessing: "Grace of the protective wings and whispered breath of angels," and his call to "the angels of the storms" to purify, cleanse, and protect his patient.

"Yes," said Adam. "Angels is one name for them; the fey would be another. You will meet them, too, in due course, but for now the hour is getting late. Do you have any final questions?"

There were two more. I wanted to know why Adam had vomited, seemingly so intentionally, and about the herbs he had given the old woman to drink.

"Ah yes, vomiting. Quite repulsive in our culture, isn't it? As if we should keep the badness inside and never let it be seen by others—and thereby increase our own suffering by holding inside that which needs to escape!

"In my tradition, we do not call it vomiting. It is a purge, a form of confession, if you will. Having absorbed the sins of my patient, these energies must be released now that they are no longer a part of her and not mine to keep.[12]

"Were I to hold on to them, two things are possible. Firstly, I might become ill myself if those energies were out of step with my own, as they were with hers.

"Secondly, however, what if those energies were a perfect match for my own and gave me added strength and power? Then, through my attachment to them, I might become hungry for more and for increasing power. I might become, that is, a soul thief; a vampire whose only reason for healing is to absorb the spirits of others. It is a real possibility and an illness among healers that they can grow dependent on their patients for their own well-being, and then they do not serve God but steal from others and work with a darkened heart. That is the way of *gwr cyfarwydd* [sorcerers], not ours, or we may become consumed by the spirits we, in turn, consume.

"There are many ways to cleanse our souls; mine is simply to purge and offer the energy to the plants to do with as they feel best. You noticed that I also used salt. This is part of the sin eater's hidden art, because salt is a perfect cleanser and an aid to the purge.

---

12 For information on the use of purging in other countries, see my book *Plant Spirit Shamanism*.

"When energies like those I released are given back to the plants, it is evident when they have been accepted because the leaves of those plants and their flowers turn black. It is evident as well when that energy has been transmuted because the plants return to their natural and beautiful state. In the between-times, those plants deserve our utmost respect, attention, and care."

I had one final question since the hour was, indeed, running late. "And the potion you gave her to take away?"

"I am glad you reminded me of that," said Adam. He walked to the kitchen and returned with an identical bottle. "How well do you know your Bible?" he asked.

Thankfully it was a rhetorical question, because I had given as much attention to the Bible, I suspect, as most young people my age: little or none.

"Psalm 51:7: 'Cleanse me with hyssop, and I will be clean.' John 19:29–30: 'A jar of wine vinegar was there, so they soaked a sponge in it, put the sponge on a stalk of the hyssop plant, and lifted it to Jesus's lips. When he had received the drink, Jesus said, "It is finished." With that, he bowed his head and gave up his spirit.'

"In this bottle there is a blend of herbs, chief amongst them hyssop, with vinegar and honey. It is not an entirely pleasant taste—though more so than some others—but its job is not to be pleasant. It is to restore balance to the soul by removing residual energies and opening the patient to grace.

"Since you have been in the presence of sin today, I want you to drink this, too, as I will, and we will cleanse ourselves together."

With that, he removed the stopper and we both drank. True to his word, it was not the most pleasant of drinks, but I did feel strangely cleansed by it and I slept better that night than I had for many.

WE CONSIDER OURSELVES a sophisticated planet in terms of modern healthcare and drug therapy, and more folkloric practices like Adam's we regard as the beliefs of heathens and the naïve, yet, even today, plant medicines are still used four times as often as "conventional" drugs throughout the world, according to the World Health Organization. UNICEF also records that 80 percent of the world's population lives in developing countries, and only 15 percent of them rely on modern medicine. Plant spirit healing is still the world's predominant practice; in this sense, it is we pill-poppers who are abnormal.

Even so, our pills and potions are derived in the main from plant extracts, too, and so, through the auspices of packaging, marketing, and stealth, we are all still modern heathens, suit-wearing savages quoting the prescriptions of doctors and scientists instead of sages and shamans but really just "primitives" ourselves, still relying on the spirits of the plants for our actual well-being.[13]

It has always been this way. The craft of the herbalist dates back at least 4,000 years—well before the nineteenth-century medical "revolution"—and even now our research is still proving the effectiveness of age-old cures. Among Adam's other natural prescriptions, for example, was the juice of willow leaves for fevers. Today, we use drugs containing salicylic acid for the same purpose instead—an extract of willow that is simply repackaged.

For practitioners of folk medicine, it is not the chemical effects of plants and herbs that fight disease or create good health, it is the spiritual intention of the plant. Every plant is a conscious intelligence whose purpose is to heal through its interaction with human beings—and which must therefore be appealed to and treated with respect.

Peony is an example. Peonies are among the earliest medicinal plants, able to cure mental illnesses, nightmares, and epilepsy, it is said, as well as control storms and protect against spirits. In

---

13   For more information on the uses of plant medicines, see the Traditional Medicine Fact Sheet produced by the World Health Organization, at http://www .who.int/mediacentre/factsheets/fs134/en/ (current as of March 24, 2008), or my book *Plant Spirit Shamanism: Traditional Techniques for Healing the Soul* (Destiny Books, 2006).

shamanic cures, it is not necessary to ingest them, only to come into contact with their purpose. Thus, they may be held like a wand over the sufferer or used to gently beat the patient like the chapaca of an Amazonian medicine man or the bundle of leaves used by Adam, each contact with the patient's body absorbing and removing a part of the illness.

Digging them up is a hazardous affair, however. The healer must only ever do so after two days of fasting and prayer, and after leaving an offering to the earth in place of the plant itself (Adam, for reasons I am unsure of, recommended goat's cheese for peonies). To do otherwise would put the healer at risk, since the peony would shriek on being pulled from the ground and anyone who heard its cry would die within days. The safest option, in fact, was to tie the plant to the tail of a dog and then call the dog to you so the plant was uprooted as the dog moved away.

Adam's belief, common among the Celtic nations, was that illness was caused by a spirit which the sufferer had brought on himself in some way by being in the presence of sin. The cure for such illness was twofold: to remove the sin and then to administer a plant which had an appropriate intention to fight off the disease.

American Indian concepts of disease and cure are similar. The Tonkawas, Comanches, and Apaches all know that the spirits of the dead, particularly if they have been sinned against in some way (for example, if burial rites are not properly conducted), can bring illness and misfortune. Only by wearing bags of herbs next to the skin can one ward off these "hungry ghosts," or by the medicine man administering floral and sweat baths to remove the illness caused by such spirits.

These herbal cures have a magical component too, working with concepts similar to the European Doctrine of Signatures[14] and the notion that "like will cure like." Thus Comanche medicine men would use snakeroot as an anti-venom, as well as applying a piece of the attacking snake itself, after it had been captured and killed, to the wound. In a similar way, Adam might recommend trefoil (a plant with heart-shaped leaves) to treat love sickness and emotional problems, and birthwort (a plant with womb-shaped flowers) to ease the pain of childbirth.

By extension, the Doctrine of Signatures means that other things besides plants can be used to heal provided they have their origins in nature, and often this was necessary, since folk medicine tends to be practiced in rural communities where people have to make the most of what is at hand. Thus, Adam would incorporate items into his cures such as soot from a fire, mud

---

14   For information on the Doctrine of Signatures, see my book *Plant Spirit Shamanism* or visit the *Vibration Magazine* website at www.floweressencemagazine.com. The direct link, http://www.floweressencemagazine.com/nov02/doctrineof signatures.html, was current as of March 24, 2008.

from a field (used in herbal plasters to soothe insect bites, etc.), vinegar for sunburn, and stones to rub over and so remove warts (the stones—as many as there are warts—are then buried at a crossroads).

Magical words, payers, and incantations were a part of his cures, too, in order to "wake up" the spirit of the plant or object he was working with. Sometimes these were personally inspired and creative, based on his connection to the spirit he was working with; others had a biblical root. It was not the words that mattered per se but the *power* of the words he used, which were employed to guide the spirits so they understood their purpose and to empower them with the authority of the healer to go about their work.

In essence, this is *faith* healing, since there is no medically known curative effect from many of these treatments—or, at least, and perhaps more accurately, modern science has not yet discovered (or re-discovered) these effects—but, then, faith, according to Adam, was the most powerful healer of all.

As I left the sin eater's cottage that night, it seemed to me that a new chapter had opened between us as a result of the day's events and the healing I had witnessed. Whatever that new chapter was, I looked forward to it, and I felt very peaceful as I began my gentle walk home beneath the moon and a sky full of stars.

As I closed his garden gate, the plants behind me, where Adam had purged, rocked to and fro in the night breeze as if holding themselves and keening, their sad and heroic leaves, I imagined, becoming darker and ever more withered.

7

Jacob's Ladder

❖ Taking one of the stones of the place, he put it under his head and lay down in that place to sleep. And he dreamed that there was a ladder set up on the earth, and the top of it reached to heaven; and behold, the angels of God were ascending and descending... Then Jacob awoke from his sleep and said, "Surely the LORD is in this place; and I did not know it."

Genesis 28:11–19

ADAM GREETED ME at his gate. It was nearing autumn of the year in which I had left school and, during the long, hot summer, I had spent quite a few days in Adam's company as I waited to join the college where I would be studying for A-levels in English, sociology, and art.

That summer I had become intrigued by the nature of sin and healing, and Adam had enjoyed teaching me about plants and introducing me further to the philosophy of the sin eater. Today, he had asked me to arrive early and, without explanation, to not sleep the night before. I arrived at his gate feeling tired but full of adventure.

"I thought we would introduce you to the art of dreaming, through which you can learn a great deal more about sin and the spirits than I can teach you," he said. "I know it has become a subject which fascinates you!"

He led me towards the stream, by now a trickle of water continually feeding the sun, and showed me the "dreaming bed" he had prepared for me. Despite any magical properties it might have, to me it looked like a patch of ferns with a "pillow" at its head fashioned from a stone.

"It's more comfortable than it looks!" he assured me. "The moss on the stone makes a fine padding, and you'll find that the shape holds your head like your mother's arms!"

I doubted it.

"I thought this dreaming would interest you, because I know that you are about to begin your studies in English literature, and there are many wonderful poets who have received their inspiration from a bed such as this.

"Wales, as you know, is the kingdom of bards and has a fine tradition of dreaming. These bards, in the old ways, would lie down next to a stream like this, their heads on a stone, and find their pace within nature, then close their eyes and drift among the stars, calling for their muse.

"The trick was to sleep-but-not-sleep, finding the betwixt-and-between that is not escape from the world but purposeful dreaming. They set their intentions to find an answer to a question which called them and to receive an inspiration: literally, a breathing-in of spirit. As you might imagine from this, slow, deep breaths and a relaxed state of mind were important. Then their dreaming would lead them to the otherworld, where the wisdom of the immortals and the unseen may be tapped.

"Perhaps you have heard of Henry Thoreau, an American dreamer and poet, and also a nature boy? Of course, he was a

Welshman in spirit! In his poem *Rumors from an Aeolian Harp*,
he writes that

> *There is a vale which none hath seen,*
> *Where foot of man has never been,*
> *Such as here lives with toil and strife,*
> *An anxious and a sinful life.*
>
> *There every virtue has its birth,*
> *Ere it descends upon the earth,*
> *And thither every deed returns,*
> *Which in the generous bosom burns.*

"He is describing *annwyn*, the otherworld of the soul and
imagination, where 'every virtue has its birth' because nothing
can exist, can be created or built, without the act of dreaming
it first. Not even this cottage, this garden—or you!—got here
without someone's dream of it!

"The Aeolian harp, by the way, was the instrument of Aeolus,
the god of the wind. It is not played by human hands but by the
air itself, so its melodies are never those of the player but are the
inspirations of nature.

"The sun is beautiful today and the air is gentle, so you should
have no trouble finding sleep and dreaming, especially if you followed my instructions to not sleep last night. I also have a gift
for you which will aid you in your task."

With that, he handed me a glass of amber liquid. "This is a dreaming brew," he said, "used in Welsh tradition for seeking a muse who can provide an answer to our questions. It was, I believe, much prized by the poets, and so it should appeal to you.

"Its basis is meddyglyn, to which has been added hops for restful sleep, elder flowers for clairvoyance and for contacting the devas and the fey, and, most importantly, Good Saint John, a fine dreaming herb indeed. Its ancient name, *fuga daemonum*, referred to its power of driving away demons and spirits, and for this reason, it is also placed beneath pillows to ward off night-mares, to be rid of enchantments, and so we may dream the faces of our future lovers..."

I sipped the brew as I listened, but as interesting as Adam's depositions on the plants and their magical powers could often be, I found it difficult to keep my eyes open, and I am sure that was really his intention: to lull me halfway to sleep by speaking slowly, quietly, and in detail about this one special plant, just as he had done before on our walk to the holy oak. If so, his scheme worked, and I missed a lot of what he said. What I know of St. John's Wort now, in fact, comes mostly from subsequent conver-sations with Adam or from my own research.

"The magic of St. John's Wort can also be understood from its other name, hypericum, which has its roots the Greek *hyper*, meaning 'over,' and *eikon*, meaning an 'icon,' because it was hung over religious images to protect the faithful in prayer.

"The Christians renamed it, of course, but even they got it partly right when they consecrated it to St. John the Baptist, because, when squashed, the flowers make a red juice which, they concluded, was because the saint's blood had fallen on the plant when he was beheaded. Because of this red color, we know that St. John's Wort will cure maladies of the blood.

"If you hold a leaf of Good St. John up to the sun, you will also see that it contains hundreds of tiny holes. By looking through it, therefore, you can find a way from darkness back to the light of God. For this reason, it helps to remind us of our purpose and will release us from the darkness of illusion and depression and restore us to love and hope.

"Finally, it is a plant that can help to change fate. A virgin who picks it on the morning of St. John's Eve, for example, will marry within a year, of that there is no doubt; while a married woman who gathers it will be pregnant within a year. But anyone sleeping with this plant beneath their pillow will invite the saint to appear and bless them in dreams, and so I also have a piece of the plant for your head."

Seeing that I was growing ever more sleepy, Adam paused for a moment and asked me to finish my drink, which I did. "Now, these instructions I am about to give you are quite precise, so pay attention," he continued.

"Every healer must make an ally in nature before any healing can be done. This ally is your first contact with the spirit world and will act as your guide, your ambassador, and your emissary. Through it, you will be introduced to the world of nature and find other allies who can assist you in many ways.

"When you have an ally in nature, for example, you may visit it in dreams to know what herbs to prescribe for a patient or what needs to be done to heal them. You may take the advice of your ally on where your journeys should lead you next. There is nothing more powerful than nature, and once you know its spirit, there is no limit to the help you may receive.

"Your first step in dreaming your ally, then, is to state your intention: that you will meet with your ally in dream-space. When that is done, let the ally guide you in answer to these greater questions ...

"When you sat by this stream some months ago, you were shown the purpose of your soul. *Knowing* your purpose is not enough, however. To live fully, you must also know what will stop you from living that purpose.

"Human beings make many excuses—lack of time, money, energy—all of which prevent them from being true to their purpose. What they really mean is that they make their own blockages—which usually amount to a fear of owning their power. Then, before they know it, their lives have slipped away, and it is too late for them to act because they are caught in the web of lies. You are still young, however, so you still have a shot at freedom before you really get caught by the world.

"And so, your questions to your ally are these: 'What will stop me from living my purpose? What are my fears, and how will I overcome them?' Are you clear on the questions?"

I nodded.

"Then lie down and sleep, and invite your dreams to answer. And let another of Thoreau's poems guide you into dreams."

Great God, I ask for no meaner pelf
Than that I may not disappoint myself
That in my action I may soar as high
As I can now discern with this clear eye ...

That my weak hand may equal my firm faith
And my life practice what my tongue saith
That my low conduct may not show
Or my relenting lines
That I thy purpose did not know
Or overrated thy designs.[15]

---

15   Excerpted from his poem "Prayer."

Adam was correct: the ferns beneath me and the mossy stone pillow were more comfortable than they appeared, and with the sun on my face and the sound of the stream like a lullaby, I drifted into sleep.

When I awoke, it was dark. I jumped to my feet, startled that the day had passed without me. I had no recollection of any dreams, just a dull headache from being out in the sun for hours and a chill in my bones now that night had descended.

I half expected to find Adam watching over me, but he was nowhere to be seen, so, stretching myself, I walked towards the cottage.

It felt as if I was walking through mud. Every step I took, the door of the cottage got farther away, and my legs were tired and numb from cold hours of inactivity.

Finally, I made it to the door and went inside. What greeted me was extraordinary: Adam dressed in green, with clothes that looked like ivy winding around him. He stood before the fire as shadows danced around and from within him. He seemed to speak in ivy too. It emerged from his mouth in great lyrical threads, wrapping itself around his head and turning orange in the glow of the fire. Every leaf was a poem, confused and breaking free of its form, landing at my feet.

There is a vale where fear has its birth
Where everything on Earth and every deed returns
Where every dead leaf burns
Where I disappoint myself
Where I lose faith
Where my low conduct shows
Where my purpose is not known

I was entangled by words. They grew up my legs like vines and found my mouth until I was choking on leaves of poems and reciting them over and over:

I disappoint myself
My purpose is not known
I disappoint myself
My purpose is not known

I tried to find new and better words, but every time I thought I'd found them, the ivy wrapped them up and choked them. Just then, Adam—now made entirely of leaves—stepped forward, I imagined to help me.

Instead, he simply pointed. With that, a wind blew through the cottage, and I felt icy hands grabbing my legs. I looked down at a swarm of creatures, some half-human–half-animal, some half-human–half-plant, who began to drag me into the shadows. I resisted, and the world exploded into fragments.

I woke up on the grass by the stream and realized that I had been dreaming after all, and now it was dark. I jumped to my feet, startled that the day had passed without me, and with a chill in my bones now that night was here.

I half expected to find Adam there but he was nowhere to be seen, so I walked towards his cottage, feeling as if I was walking through mud. Something about this felt familiar, and then I realized I'd lived it before. I looked down and saw why I found it so hard to move: I was held by creatures, some half-human—half-animal, some half-human—half-plant.

This time I awoke in a cave, though it felt more like the inside of a tree: organic and living. I knew this feeling as well, but I couldn't remember where from. There was something on my face, dry and chalky. I ran my tongue over it and it tasted of charcoal, bark, and salt: soot, or maybe ash.

The half-creatures grabbed me again and led me to a cauldron bubbling on a fire. My head was pushed forward to look inside. There were bones and lumps of flesh: my bones and flesh, I realized, as I looked at myself—the one who was watching—and saw that I was nothing but charcoal. Strangely, I felt no fear, no panic, nor even interest. The experience was totally nonemotional.

And then in the waters, reflected, I saw the image of the most beautiful woman standing right behind me. She was dressed in white, with daisy chains in her hair and around her wrists and ankles. Her eyes were the deepest green and her hair long and black. "My name is Rachel," she said, "and my gift to you is the rose, the most beloved of the prophets. Tell me what you see in the waters."

"My body dissolving," I said.

"Ah—then you must look harder."

Reflected in the waters, faintly at first but with increasing clarity, I saw that there was something more: a ladder behind us, going up into the chimney of the cave or the hollow trunk of the tree.

On the first rung was one of the creatures I had seen earlier. Its face was contorted in fear. "I am a sinner, and I have been sinned against," it intoned over and over, hugging itself in terror and looking warily around as if it expected persecution, or worse, to emerge from the shadows and claim it at any moment.

On the second rung was another, more human creature. It looked puzzled, as if pondering a truth. "What is right and wrong?" it asked aloud. "How real can our sins be?"

On the third rung was another. "What I call 'sin' is my investment in pain," it said. "There is no sin in the world, only my attachments and projections. Everything is perfect as it is."

On the next rung was another, more human still. A light shone around it, and it seemed able to speak without words.

"The world is illusion. All is love. God loves us despite our 'sins'; otherwise, he could not love himself."

This insight was answered by another from the rung above, that "'God' himself is an illusion: an attachment and a projection of need. Who else can have the experience I have? Therefore, *I* must be God, and *I* choose to sin or not sin."

"There is no sin," said the creature on the next rung. "Everything is perfect; all we need to do is appreciate our own perfection."

The ladder dissolved into the waters of the cauldron, and I turned to face Rachel. "It is the ladder of evolution," she said, "of our thoughts and understanding of ourselves; of our journeys from a low state of wisdom to our knowledge of truth: that we are here as the agents of God.

"Once you know this truth—not *think* it, but *know* it—you will have found your place in the web of dreams," she added, putting her finger to my lips. "Then you will understand that you—and every living thing—are no less a god than God himself.

"So tell me, what is it that you fear and which stops you from being who you are?"

"If I am God, then I am afraid of my own perfection," I answered. "If I have infinite choice, then I am responsible for all that I do. There is no situation I can hide behind or hide from. I am responsible for it all."

She smiled approvingly, as if I had given the only correct answer to some great cosmic puzzle. "You are here on Earth to play," she said, "to experience, explore, and find love—and all that we/you ask is that you act responsibly so you do not hurt yourself or others. God knows that even this is far from easy, but, in times of doubt, I am here to help you."

With that, I felt myself dragged to the ground and my body of soot and charcoal was ripped apart and shredded. It felt perfectly natural, expected even, and there was no pain. The surgery continued as my bones and skin, boiled dry in the cauldron, were put back in its place. At the end, I lay relaxed but exhausted on the floor of the cave-tree, the cauldron empty of flesh and the cavity of my chest and stomach held open.

"This is my gift to you so you can find me whenever you are in need," said Rachel. Millions of rose petals rained down on me then, caressing my face, drifting into my mouth, and filling the cavity of my chest until I became a thing made of petals. Only then was my body sealed.

Rachel leaned forward and kissed me on the lips. "Remember: I am always here," she said, and then she became the shadows.

I awoke, and it was dark. I thought I felt petals, but wiping my eyes I realized that I was staring at the earth with a fern across my face. I stumbled to my knees and straight into sunlight, which dazzled me with its brilliance.

"Lie still, relax," said Adam, who had been there to watch over me throughout my dreams, it seemed, and to greet me on my return. "Regain your senses. You have a little while before the thing that calls us next."

I remained still, breathing deeply and looking up at the clouds, wondering how their shapes could change so quickly, from something I knew without doubt to be a spark, a planet, a ridiculous dog chasing its tail, a serpent, or a face, to a footprint in moon dust or a rose, all in the space of a heartbeat.

"Impermanence," I heard Rachel say. "You make the moment; the heartbeat is yours, and you are the one who gives meaning."

"You realized that you are powerful," said Adam, "that we are not sent here to do God's work without the ability to do so—and that with our power comes our greatest fear: we are responsible for ourselves."

I nodded. That, indeed, and in a nutshell, was what I now knew.

"Good. Then that is the lesson. And now I want you to confess."

Before me, Adam had laid out a tray. To the right was a bowl of water, to the left a bowl of ashes, and in the middle a single white candle, a sheet of paper, and a pen.

"Confession, as the saying goes, is good for the soul—and so it is!" he said. "When we hold on to energies which do not serve us—our fears, our guilt, the memories of the times we have 'failed' (by which I actually mean that we have tested our love in the realm of experience and learned something of value)—we prevent ourselves from engaging with the flow of life and from living our purpose in full.

"In front of you is a bowl of water. Dab a little on your face.

"Also before you is a bowl of ashes. In a moment, I will ask you to 'confess'—that is, to write out your 'sins' as you see them: all the times you have allowed illusion to stand between you and the truth of your perfection, or allowed fear to overrule your soul's intention to love—and you should know that this bowl of ashes contains the confessions of all those people I have heard across the years who had the same fear as you. You are far from alone.

"Every sin eater carries these ashes with him, and the only time they are ever offered back to the earth is when that healer dies, unless they are gifted to another who will carry on the work. Take a handful of ashes and rub them on your face."

I did so, and the dampness of the water held them so they became a sort of mask.

"Good. Now take the pen and paper, and write out all the times you have not been true to your purpose because you have allowed fear—of being seen, of being judged, of making yourself vulnerable, of taking responsibility—to stand in the way of your truth. You have eleven minutes. You will find it a start, at least!"

I wrote in a stream of consciousness, and it seemed that as soon as I started I could hardly stop. I never realized I had been so fearful of the opinions of others before Adam's permission to say so. When he told me to stop, it was as if I had hardly begun.

"That will do for now," he said. "You can always return to this practice and, indeed, I recommend it.

"For now, I want you to burn the paper you have written on. As you do so, see all of your fears released, flying free from the page as if on angel's wings, while you make a silent commitment to be free of them and never to sin against yourself again."

I placed the paper in the candle flame and watched as it became cinders.

"Now add your ashes to the bowl so that others may learn from you. As I said, you are not the first and you will not be the last to share the same fear of living."

The bowl was almost full. So many ashes, so many fears, and all of them the same: the fear of simply being, of acknowledging who we are and stepping into our power, our birthrights as the "sons of God" on Earth.

"Good," said Adam. "And now for the next thing! You will like this because you get to ask lots of questions! Or, rather, since it's been a long day for you, let me answer them for you without your needing to ask! But first take off your shirt and shoes."

I removed my clothing, which felt wonderful. The sun caressed my skin and the breeze played lightly across my body so I felt warm and cool and comfortable all at once.

"In Wales you will find a thousand holy wells, all of which possess strange powers," said Adam, "or, rather, they are not strange at all but perfectly natural, although, for some odd reason, we regard the natural as strange these days. Some of these wells are for healing, some for cursing, and there are wells which make the poor rich, the unhappy happy, and the unlucky lucky. The Wells of St. Mary—the *Ffynnon Fair*—are the greatest and purest of all, and are guarded by dragons and angels.

"In this bucket is the water of the Ffynnon Fair, to which has been added flowers of absolution: polemonium—also known as Jacob's ladder—for insight; heartsease for the sorrows of the soul; holy leaf for blessings; honesty for all things true; and rue for casting out fears.

"What we are about to do is a baptism. I will pour these waters over you so you are returned to a pure and sinless state and become once again unformed. Your sins and your fears will no longer exist. You may believe this absolutely: having made your confession, you are free to start again.

"This will also be an action of grace, therefore, and of forgiveness—not from me, but *from yourself to yourself*. You will receive these waters and forgive the sins you have made against your soul, so you may learn and grow from them—and, well, let yourself off the hook for being a dumb bastard like the rest of us!"

With that, he poured the cold waters over me three times, and with each gasp as the chill of the water hit me, I breathed in the scent and spirit of the flowers of forgiveness until I felt myself awake and whole again.

"Good," said Adam. "Everything is now as it should be."

He handed me a towel, and making his way back to the cottage, told me to dry myself off and come in when I was ready. I took my time, standing in the garden, feeling warm and refreshed and blessed as the sun smiled down on my skin.

My own smile lasted all the way to the cottage, until I opened the door and saw her—dressed in white, with deep green eyes and shining black hair—sitting on Adam's couch, absorbed in a magazine.

"This is Rachel," said Adam. "She arrived today while you were dreaming, and she'll be staying with us for a while."

Rachel looked up and smiled. It was the same smile I had seen in my dream.

8

The Visible Face of Spirit

❖ Angelic minds, they say, by simple intelligence
Behold the Forms of nature. They discern
Unerringly the Archetypes, all the verities
Which mortals lack or indirectly learn.

C. S. Lewis,
"On Being Human"

THERE WAS AN obvious explanation, of course—although the obvious is never the only explanation or even, necessarily, the right one.

Rachel was the student of Adam's friend David, an herbalist in the town of Adam's birth. David had a more orthodox approach to the plants than Adam and thought it might therefore interest Rachel to spend a few weeks with his friend so she could see a different side of nature and learn the folklore of the herbs she was using. David had, in any case, been a little under the weather of late, and Rachel thought it would be good for him to have a break from her.

Arrangements had been made accordingly, and Rachel had arrived that morning. The only person who hadn't been consulted, it appeared, was me—not that it was necessary, I suppose, since discussions between Adam and his friends were really none of my concern.

Adam thought it would be good for me as well to have the company of someone closer to my own age, instead of "an old man who's constantly following you about and insisting on strange practices and lectures about 'sin' at every turn."

Rachel was actually a little older than me (years mean everything when you're young). I was, at this time, close to my seventeenth birthday, while she had just celebrated her twentieth. She was bright, sunny, and smart, and I liked her immediately.

Adam, true to form, however, was more interested in the synchronicity of our meeting after I had related my experiences to him: of my "dreaming Rachel"—an ally he had sent me to find—and her appearance on his doorstep at the very time that I was dreaming. He grew even more excited (and I grew more amazed) when he discovered that Rachel's second name was Rose, the plant ally that the Rachel of my dreams had given me.

"There are no accidents!" he declared. "Both of you, if you track back over your lives, will realize that this meeting between the three of us was as inevitable as the sunrise.

"Your move here from the city," he said to me, "is responsible for your finding me, and through that for finding Rachel, who is on the same path as you, in her own way.

"Rachel, by finding David, it was quite inevitable that you would meet me and, through that, that you would find Ross. In this way, our little group has always existed—before today only in the mind of God, perhaps, or in our immaterial dreams—but now we have made it form through the workings of chance.

"And so, you see, chance is not random, and there is no coincidence. Chance is the dreaming of God, and had we looked for the signs before, we would all have known this moment before it arose. The Creator has made a book of nature for us to read these signs of our futures; it was just that we didn't look.

"Since chance has brought us together in this way, however, today is the perfect time for us to pay attention to the auguries of fate and to explore nature's omens to see what else is in store for the three of us!"

The Voice of Nature

THERE WAS A diviner in the hills of Wales who was called upon one day by a man who wished to know the future. He arrived at the diviner's cottage on a Thursday evening to hear if the time was auspicious for him to make a journey and do business with a merchant in the east.

The diviner listened to the man's enquiry and agreed to help but immediately sent him away, telling him to return at noon exactly—no earlier and no later—on the following Monday. Then he would have his answer.

The diviner did nothing for the next few days, but on Monday at dawn—an unusual hour for him—he arose and dressed.

Now, I say "dressed," but half-dressed would be more accurate. He put on his trousers but not his shirt. He wore a hat but no socks. He half-shaved and half-washed and then went to the kitchen, where he drank half a cup of tea and ate half of his breakfast. Then he opened the door of his cottage and stood in the doorway, neither in nor out.

He closed his eyes and turned three times, then opened one eye and saw what he saw: a bird flying across the dawning sky from the west.

He closed his eyes again and turned another three times, now in the opposite direction, then opened his other eye and saw what he saw: a tree that was bending in the wind, towards the hills and away from his cottage.

He closed his eyes for a third time and again made three turns, this time in the first direction, and now he opened both eyes and saw what he saw again: a fox in his garden, watching him with suspicion.

The diviner nodded, said "Thank you," and then went back into his cottage, washed himself thoroughly, completed his shave, and dressed fully. He returned to the kitchen, finished his breakfast, and began to write the story of what he had seen.

His client arrived a few hours later and put forth his question again: "Is the time right for me to travel to the east?"

"I would not recommend it," said the diviner. "The deal you make will not be a good one, and you will lose customers. The merchant you do business with will be crooked, and for this you will be shunned when you return home by the people who have bought your products and have come to treat you with distrust."

"Thank you," said the man and left.

He never made his journey to the east.

✦ ✦ ✦

"Now, why do you suppose the diviner said those things? And what of his curious actions?" asked Adam.

Rachel and I looked blankly at each other. Adam sighed—more at me than at her, I thought, as if I should really have known better.

"The diviner arose at *dawn*—neither night nor day—on a *Monday*—neither the start of the week nor its end. He *half*-dressed, he ate *half* his food, and he stood in the *doorway* of his cottage—neither in nor out.

"He closed *one* eye and he looked out on nature three times—three is an 'incomplete' number and more open to change than 'solid' numbers like two or four—and he watched the world for signs.

"His client wanted to travel *east*, and yet the bird flew from the west. The tree bent *away* from the diviner's home, as if shunning his cottage. The fox in his garden was wary and guarded. In the context of the man's question, the auguries of nature gave the diviner an exact answer, and one which makes perfect sense. Because of this, there could be no other advice to give. Do you see?

"The way to receive these signs is to put oneself in the place of the betwixt-and-between, just as the diviner did: neither out nor in, neither dressed nor naked, neither night nor day, but always on the threshold between worlds where the spirits whisper loudest to us.

"This form of divination is called *rhamanta*—omen-seeking from nature—because nature, you see, is the visible face of spirit and will always reveal the truth to us. It will remind us of our souls and the purpose that is in them, and all we need do is listen and have faith in what we are told.

"And so your work for today is to walk out into nature with a question in mind and let it be answered for you."

The process for doing so, Adam explained, was to find a betwixt-and-between place of our own. This might be the edge of a forest, for example, where the tree line just began, and so was not the forest itself or the open field but the threshold of change from one form to another. Or it might be the bank of a stream—not water and not quite solid ground—or a gateway, the edge of a shadow, or the place where grassland met trackway through a field—"Whatever place sings to your souls"—and to ask our questions there.

We would need three such places, he said, in order to receive three different points of view, or, maybe, the same view expressed in three different ways. When we had found our places, we were to close our eyes and ask our questions, then open one eye and look around. Whatever we saw first or what called us most strongly was the augury we were to receive.

"Write down what you are told each time so you do not forget it, and when you have your information, use your imagination, as the diviner did, to create a single story that links the words of nature together.

"Rachel, you may ask any question you wish. Ross, since you are familiar with my strange ways and have already worked on finding your purpose and the things that block you from it, I have a specific question in mind for you: 'What is the most important thing I can do *now* to help me achieve my purpose?' This will be a practical thing—something you can do straightaway. It could be to join a rugby team, or pick flowers and give them to a girl. It doesn't matter to us what it is (although it may matter greatly in the eyes of spirit) as long as it is doable. What we are not interested in is the ethereal, the fluffy, the maybes.

"Sin—illusion and wandering from purpose—is released through action, through doing something to create a change, and this requires a movement of our energy into the world. This is how we bring spirit into matter: through acts of creation—

and, if they are the right acts, by creating more love in the world as a result."

Rachel and I set out for the day, across fields, hills, and flat-lands, a little embarrassed at first since we had only just met, and, as our baptism of fire, had been asked to bare our souls to each other by posing intimate questions to nature. Our shyness soon passed, however, and we began to enjoy each other's company.

We found ourselves in a wood at some point during the day. At first it was a pleasant hinterland of light and shade as the sun found us deep amongst trees, but as we ventured farther, the undergrowth became more difficult and it grew cooler and then chilled as sunlight gave way to shadow. Rather than go on, we sat down for a while and began talking about things which were far from profound: the music we liked, the films we had seen, all of it mundane and obvious—the things that young adults discuss.

It is often the case with people that even when we do not find them immediately attractive, once we get to know them and hear their thoughts and dreams, they change physically and become the most beautiful men or women in the world. I already found Rachel attractive and, as she spoke—of her love for the hills, the plants, the water, and for the solitude of the valleys—I felt my heart open and her bright spirit enter. When it was time for me to speak, I wanted no more words, only to hold her.

Perhaps she felt it too because something passed between us, as light as a spider's thread, and, in passing, touched us both. In the silence of leaves and shadows, we kissed.

If Adam was right—that this meeting had somehow been preordained by what he paradoxically called "chance"—then it was inevitable that our kiss would happen and that we would remove our clothes and make love in the forest, entwined like roots beneath the trees. I still feel that it should have happened, and that things may have been different if it had, but it was not to be. We were shocked from our rapture instead by the sound of shotgun fire and, around us, of pellets hitting branches and splintering wood. We sat up, half-dressed, and listened.

It was common for poachers to wander these woods in search of game, and it often appeared that everyone in the countryside owned a 12-bore shotgun, a mean double-barrelled rifle that made a sound like thunder when fired and sprayed shot in a wide arc. Our fear, then, was not at the sound of a gun but that perhaps the hunter had not seen us and might hit us in error, as his last shot had been frighteningly close.

We knew we couldn't get up and simply run, in case we were mistaken for game and drew lethal attention, nor did we want to stay there and risk an accidental shooting, so we compromised and began quietly and on all fours to creep through the trees, so close to the earth that its damp musk filled our lungs.

Finally we came to a place where we sensed there was enough distance between us and the hunter that we could move more quickly, and, standing, ran through the woods until we felt ourselves safe.

I caught my breath and looked up for the fist time since we had started to run, and came face-to-face with the half-rotten corpse of a fox that had been strung up in the trees, dried black blood crusted around its mouth and nose. I drew back and looked around. Other animals and birds, all of them dead and decomposing, were tied in the branches around us. We stood in a glade of death.

It is a practice in rural communities for farmers to hang the corpses of animals close to their farms so that predators such as foxes, seeing the bodies and smelling the aroma of death, are discouraged from entering the farmstead to attack animals and crops. This, however, was excessive. There was death everywhere.

It occurred to me—or to a part of me, at least—that the question Adam had set for me was what action I could take to be true to my purpose. I had no idea how this could be an answer, even though it was the first and most obvious sign I had received since the question was posed. My inclination was only to run from it, while Rachel stood horrified, almost transfixed by the death around us.

She had the same disgust as I did, however, and we quickly found a way out of the woods and onto clear land, where we could at least be seen by the hunter and not be mistaken for prey.

"What was your question to nature?" I asked her when our pulses were finally back to normal.

"About my career and my future," she said. "I want to work overseas as a volunteer to help people in the developing world, as a teacher or a doctor."

"So what did you make of what just happened?"

"I absolutely refuse to take that as any kind of a sign!" she declared. "All those dead animals around us—it was revolting!"

I wondered if that was possible—to choose one's signs selectively from nature—or whether we had to accept what was shown to us. It seemed to me the latter, but I said nothing. Instead, we walked into sunshine, both of us still dishevelled and not fully dressed after our kisses and caresses in the woods. But by now the intimate moment was over.

Crossing the field and the fence on the other side, we came to a large holly bush that, for some reason, appealed to me. I closed my eyes in the threshold-place where the shadow of the leaves fell upon the ground and turned three times, as Adam had instructed, then opened one eye. I found myself looking into the distance at the hills and, above them, at a sparrow hawk, hovering as they do when they have detected movement on the ground that might be their next meal.

I made a note of it and turned to Rachel, who had repeated the exercise alongside me. Following her gaze, I saw that she was looking at a spot much closer to us and had found an owl pellet, a white and brown lozenge-shaped package of fur and bones: the regurgitated remains of an owl's successful scavenging and feasting on mouse or shrew.

By now, we had been on our journey of omen-seeking for some hours, and it was late afternoon, so we moved ahead quickly to our next location. Drawn, as Adam would put it, by the whispers of spirit, we entered a field I knew well on our way back to the sin eater's cottage, having walked it many times with Adam. I had always liked the spot where the stream ran and the leaves of the willows—the "trees of the threshold," as Adam once called them—swayed in the breeze on the bank.

I closed my eyes there, and on opening them, a feather caught my gaze, standing point-down at an angle in the grass. Like an arrow, I thought, or, now, as I looked more closely, like a writing quill in the inkwell of some poet. I recorded my observations and sat down to prepare the story that would somehow link all three of my symbols together.

Adam had given us instructions not to think too much in our creation of this story, but to put down on paper whatever occurred to us first. So I placed my pen on the page, and, in another stream of consciousness, wrote the story of what I had seen.

> The fox, looking for food and finding the farmer's property, met with a grisly fate. The bird saw it and understood the message not to steal. It dropped a feather for others to find so they would understand too: find your own nourishment, live your own truth, and write your own story. That is the way to survive and live a full life.

I doubt it would have impressed Shakespeare. It might not impress Adam either, I thought, but it made a sort of sense to me.

My pilgrimage into nature had been to find something I could do immediately to begin living the purpose of my soul. Writing had always appealed to me, as well as the search for truth along the road less travelled—which I had certainly experienced today, in all senses of the words—and, as I looked at my writing on the page, it occurred to me that I had enjoyed the work of the day and especially putting it all together and creating the little story which was a reflection of my truth and discoveries.

There was a sense of healing in it for me—of meditation and "good medicine"—and, however subtly, I made a resolution that day that I would explore the world and write of my experiences. Perhaps I would become a journalist or a travel writer, I reasoned, as my expression of love and purpose: bringing truth and new perspectives as my healing gift to the world.

This seemed a satisfactory answer and, in any case, I was already drifting that way through my decision to study English literature and sociology, the exploration of other cultures, on my college course. Today's divination gave me confidence in that decision, and I felt more certain that the direction my life was taking was the right one for me.

Although I wasn't to know it then, for the future seemed a long way off, I did become a writer, though not of the travelogues I had imagined, but of books on other cultures, other ways of seeing, and the spiritual practices of other countries. *The Journey to You*, my first book, was published in 2001—almost a quarter of a century after that day of omen-seeking in the fields; although, in many ways, it was written from that moment because that was when my intention was set.

I wandered over to Rachel to see what she had discovered and found her gazing at a tree. It looked as if it had been hit by a tractor or some other piece of heavy machinery, because the trunk was gouged and scarred and the bark falling from it at a point along its middle.

"What do you make of that?" I asked her.

"I think it's a warning about the dangers of standing still," she said. "If you're too rooted and don't keep moving, you can get hurt because you don't get out of the way when something 'heavy' comes towards you! I'd say it's a good sign, wouldn't you, since my question was about my desire to travel and work over-seas?"

"I guess so," I replied, "if that's what it means to you. Are you going to write out your story?"

"No, I can't be bothered with that," she said. "We've done enough for today. Let's go back and have tea."

Adam had anticipated the request, and tea was already set up for us in the garden when we got there.

Over it, I told him my story and related my experiences, and he looked pleased with my discoveries. "Writing is one noble path," he said.

Rachel apologized for not bringing him her story but explained that she had been tired and still a little shocked after our encounter with the hunter and the shots going off around us. Adam seemed quite relaxed about it. She was, after all, not his student in the same way he had come to regard me, so it wasn't his place to ask too much of her.

She told him what she'd seen, however—the dead fox (which she'd now chosen to include as her first omen, despite her ear-lier resistance to the idea), the owl pellet and the mouse bones it contained, and the tractor-hit tree—and said what she thought it all meant: "Keep moving! If the fox and the mouse hadn't been caught, they wouldn't be where they are now, and if trees could move, that one would not have been hit. I'm happy to follow that advice and get travelling as soon as I can!"

I noticed that Adam looked pensive, however, as she relayed these omens to him. As she finished, a bird—a crow, I thought—cawed loudly in the field, and the distant church bell chimed five times to mark the hour. Adam's eyes narrowed and slowly and subtly took in the garden, as if looking for something in particular. Just as subtly, I followed his gaze until it came to rest on a fence post, on top of which sat a robin. It saw us watching and, disturbed by the attention, flew off.

"You know," Adam said, apparently to both of us, "the old ones knew that fate is never fixed and that chance can be changed by intention. The omens you received were in answer to specific questions and show you a probable outcome if you pursue your purpose in that particular way.

"This information from the spirit of nature does not mean that things *have* to be the way you were shown them, however, if, through an exercise of free will, you decide on another course of action and commit to that instead. Then you throw life open to chance again.

"This is called 'making a refusal.' It is not the same as 'refusing' or 'just not doing something,' which is far more passive. *Making a refusal* is having a firm intention that things will be otherwise. It is like standing with your fist raised to the sky and screaming at the top of your lungs: 'I refuse to allow this to happen!'

"The procedure for doing so is simple enough and not quite as dramatic as I just put it! Now you know the probable outcome of your current course from what nature has shown you, you simply hold that outcome in your mind as if it were already happening and track back through all the decisions and actions you have taken in your life to get to this point. Changing any one of those decisions will change the outcome of the whole. That is 'making a refusal.'"

I wondered for a moment what Adam might be getting at as I pondered the outcome I had seen for myself, but I was quite happy with my course and so, too, I thought, was Rachel.

"So be it, then!" said Adam and then, in a lighter tone, "Let me get you more tea!" He set off into the kitchen and, after a respectful few minutes, I followed him in.

"What did you see?" I asked him. "And what was that about refusals?"

"What I am about to say is not for Rachel's ears," he replied. "You understand?"

My stomach turned over, but I nodded.

"The fox, the mouse within the owl's package, the wounded tree; these were the things she saw. And, as she related them, the call of the crow—the messenger between worlds—the church bell which chimes the hour and calls the faithful to prayer, the robin, guardian of transient spirits. What do they mean to you?"

I shook my head, although my stomach still churned as if it had an answer.

"How many times did the church bell ring?" he asked.

"Five." I had counted them.

"Correct. And all of these signs together can mean only one thing: Death is coming. In five years—no more, no less—unless a refusal is made.

"For now, however, let us put all of this behind us while we have today."

We went back to the garden and drank our tea together, chatting and enjoying each other's company until the sky began to darken and it was time for me to leave.

The autumn passed, then the winter, and 1977 became 1978 before I had the chance to spend much more time with Adam. My A-level course meant that I was occupied with studies, new ideas, partying, and meeting and making new friends. By the time I saw Adam again, Rachel was long gone, having returned to Wales and the life she loved in the valleys.

Despite our easy friendship and what might have been between us, I was to see Rachel only one other time, a situation in which we never spoke. And Adam never mentioned her again.

In 1982, though, during my second year of university studies, I picked up a newspaper one day by chance. I never bought newspapers and still try to avoid them and their sad tales of conflict, greed, and fear, but a friend had bought this one and I flicked through it in his room.

There, tucked away on the inner pages, was a story about a woman who had been a volunteer in Africa, teaching English to children and young adults. She was sleeping in her room one night when she was disturbed by someone and, getting up to ask who was there, she had startled a thief—one of the young people she was there to help. He responded by stabbing her to death.

Her name was Rachel Rose, and she was twenty-five years old.

9

The Truths of Angels

> So in a voice, so in a shapeless flame,
> Angels affect us oft, and worshipp'd be;
> Still when, to where thou wert, I came,
> Some lovely glorious nothing did I see.
>
> *John Donne,*
> *"Air and Angels"*

"I PROMISED YOU years ago that one day I would take you to meet the fey folk, or, as I call them, the angels of the storms," said Adam.

I hadn't seen him for some months now that I was at college, a "man of the world" finding my own independence, and I think he recognized a change in me: a longing for experience, for wider horizons, and for more freedom than this village could give me. With the racing pulse of an eighteen-year-old ready to challenge anything and certain about everything, I had forgotten all about the promise of angels that Adam had made to a young child. But I recalled it now and sensed its importance to him, as if he wanted to make good on his word as we neared the end of our journey together.

"First of all," he said, "you need to understand the peculiar arrangement between the fairy and the Welsh." Another of his stories, I thought to myself.

"The Welsh are fugitives, forced to leave their cities during our great historic conflicts with the tribes of Persia. To defend ourselves, our magicians tamed the *simorgh*, gigantic birds large enough to carry off a whale. They had the look of an eagle about them but with the face and teeth of a wolf and the claws of a lion. Their feathers were the color of bronze, and they were avaricious in their taste for human flesh and, even more so, for the sweet tang of a mortal soul.

"The simorgh were also known as rocs and are written of in many legends. The adventurer Marco Polo described his encounter with one in the thirteenth century: 'It was for all the world like an eagle, but one indeed of enormous size; so big that its quills were twelve paces long and thick in proportion. And it is so strong that it will seize an elephant in its talons and carry him high into the air and drop him so that he is smashed to pieces; having so killed him, the bird swoops down on him and eats him at leisure.'[16]

"Through our magical powers, the simorgh agreed to defend us against our enemies.

"Terrified of these birds, the King of Persia enlisted his own sorcerers, and eventually they were able to lay an enchantment on the simorgh and turn them to fairy, doomed to live as ephemera deep within Earth.

"Now that the simorgh were no longer a danger, the Persian army laid waste to the tribes of the Welsh, and we had no choice but to retreat. We travelled, living off the land and learning the

---

16 *The Travels of Marco Polo* by Marco Polo (fourteenth-century manuscript, reprinted by Cosimo Classics in 2007). This tells the story of Venetian trader and explorer Marco Polo (1254–1324), who claimed to have found the court of Kublai Khan and served the emperor as his emissary. It relates his journeys to the lands of Cathay, his firsthand accounts of the wonders of ancient China, and the tales of Arab travelers that Polo heard along the Silk Road.

magic of herbs, until we came to Russia, then Spain, and then through France to Wales, where we settled as the first race of Britain.

"Every step of the way, the simorgh came with us, bound to the Welsh through their peculiar destiny, making their homes in the land and the trees and the rivers of Wales, and, from there, to the highlands and moors of Britain.

"So, you see, 'fairies' are not something twee and biddable; once they were giants, and they can be warriors, fierce and frightening, who know the light and shade and taste of the soul. You may also consider them mercenaries, fighting for their purpose, which is freedom and the return to their original form so that they, too, can evolve beyond their enchantment.

"What they will never do is acquiesce to your bidding like some genie from a bottle. But if you make them your friends, you will find no stronger or more loyal allies. This is why I call them 'angels' and their tempestuous nature is why I refer to them as creatures of the storms. They are the natural energies of the earth. They help with our healing work and can summon the air and the elements to blow through us, carrying away illness and illusion as if a gale was howling in our souls.

"The way to meet them for the first time is at night, and we must prepare for our encounter thoroughly."

He sent me off to gather plants—marigolds, rose petals, wild thyme, hazel bark, hollyhocks, St. John's Wort, and nettles—while he filled a tub with water, adding a dash or two of perfume, a few drops of vinegar, and, finally, a pinch of tobacco and a little rum.

"This is the recipe for seeing the angels," he said as he stirred the mixture, "apart, that is, from Good Saint John, which is for our protection against abduction. I am adding a little of the ash from your confession as well, to show that we are pure in spirit and come with good intentions."

When the mix was prepared, we undressed to our shorts and Adam poured the water over me, asking me to turn three times as he did so to increase the power of the charm, and to breathe deeply so I took in the spirit of the plants as he tipped the water over my head and it cascaded down my body. The last instruction was easy to follow as the water was icy cold and made me gasp. "Breathe out forcefully as well, to release negativity. Scream or shout if you want to!"

When I had been bathed and poured the water for Adam, we allowed the sun to dry us and then dressed ourselves again. "If any herbs remain on your skin, leave them there; it is a good sign," said Adam, "especially the nettles. They will heat your body and provide the boiling energy you need for clearer sight.

"Now we must rest and make our prayers. Do not eat for the rest of the day and try, if you can, not to engage with any living soul except in this one thing: to tell your parents that you will be staying out tonight and also to ask if, in a few days, you may spend some time in Wales with a friend of yours. We have a journey ahead of us."

Adam told me to return at 11 PM and, with that, I made my way home and rested, as he had said to do.

When I returned, Adam was waiting for me with two short staffs, a foot or so in length, fashioned, he said, from a single branch of the rowan [mountain ash] tree—one for him and one for me. "We will carry these with us for protection," he said. "Witches have a great fear of the ash, and anyone who carries *pen cerdin* is quite safe from their spells. In Wales, it was once common for people to carry a twig of mountain ash on any journey at night, the origin of these wands being not to *make* magic but to deflect it."

He handed me the ash wand, and we walked out into the fields.

"Moving at night requires an attitude of stillness," said Adam, "and new ways of seeing, since angels always appear first at the edges of our vision—the betwixt-and-between of our sight, if you will: the place between seeing and not-seeing. This, in fact, is how all spirits will come to you: you will see them first from the corners of your eyes."

There are many ways of seeing, according to Adam. The first and least useful is normal sight, where, in the case of most people, the eyes are fixed on the ground and the attention so limited that we miss 90 percent of what is right in front of us.

Gazing is a different way of looking at the world, where the foreground and background become reversed, and it is possible to see things we normally overlook. This was the method we had been practicing during the months of our work together. It involved making the eyes soft and slowing down to nature's pace so that awareness and attention expanded and new details emerged from the environment.

Then there was "peripheral" or *spirit-vision*, the method he recommended for seeing angels and for becoming a part of nature itself. This was wide-angle vision, which involved deliberately taking the awareness to the periphery of our arc of sight, so we continued to look ahead but gave most attention to what we saw from the corners of our eyes. Spirit-vision is also the form used by most animals and by trackers, as it gives a wider field of awareness and is good for detecting the movements of predators or prey.

The last of the four "attitudes of seeing" that Adam taught me was *focusing*: narrowing the eyes to truly study something at close range, which might also involve making tunnels of the hands to cut out peripheral sights.

The first type of vision—*lack* of awareness—he discounted almost entirely as being of such limited value that it was only really useful in situations where we didn't want to be present and where we therefore put our bodies on "automatic pilot," which accounted, he said, for its common usage in cities and towns.

It is "normal vision" as we understand it, as if our nervous systems are set to automatic so that our primal survival mechanisms are all that is left of us, and our minds and spirits are elsewhere. It is what enables us to walk through crowds of people without really looking at where we are going or being present in our surroundings. It is the attitude we see on the streets every day.

We can get so wrapped up in being elsewhere, however, that even this skill can let us down, hence our tendency sometimes to walk out in front of traffic without paying attention to our own safety or where we are. "Normal vision" can therefore be an agent of spiritual—or literal—death.

The other three ways of seeing have value and application, however, especially for merging with nature and opening to spirit. Adam's practice for developing these was to have me close my eyes and then stare into the darkness beneath my eyelids as if it was a real scene I was looking at. This was focusing, bringing the eyes into an attitude of looking with real intent. It produces a muscular change in and around the eyes that can be felt.

From this position, we can soften the eyes into gazing, which will also have the effect of slowing the breath so we relax into the scene and its full sensory meaning starts to emerge.

Finally, we allow the eyes, still closed, to widen into spirit-vision. This feels like a theater curtain is opening and produces a muscular change as well, so we are taken deeper into the scene before us.

The last stage is to open the eyes and to find ourselves looking at the landscape with much wider and more relaxed vision, attentive to detail in front of and to the sides of us without being focused completely on, or overly occupied by, any of it. The mood it evokes is one of blending, as if we are connected to the environment and it is moving through us as much as we through it; as if we are *a part* of nature, not *apart* from it, in Adam's words.

We continued walking in spirit-vision for an hour or so, until we entered a field in which blue lights seemed to hover just above the ground. This was our final destination.

Our position at the edge of the field was slightly elevated, and from this perspective, I could see that some of these lights made distinct groups of circles, while others snaked serpent-like through the grass from group to group. A few of them stood alone. I didn't know what to make of this and asked Adam what I was seeing.

"You have heard of so-called fairy rings," he answered. "Most people quaintly think that these are rings left by fairies as a result of their meetings; in fact, they are the means of *meeting* the fairies. As we get closer, you will see."

We set out for the first group, which, interestingly, began to lose its glow as we got nearer, as if hiding from us. Stalking through the darkness of the night, we arrived at the spot from which the glow had originated, and I saw that they were not lights at all but small groups of mushrooms, two to four inches high, with thin stems and conelike heads, each with a small, round peak at its tip.

"You see the shape of their heads are like caps," said Adam. "That is why people mistook them for fairies and why those of the fey are often drawn or painted as little people wearing pointed hats.

"In fact, it would be better to look at the cave paintings of our ancestors if you want to understand the nature of these mushrooms. Such paintings often show wise men working with these forces of nature to aid them in prophecy, healing, and spirit-flight, for mushrooms like these are plants of power and vision. They open a doorway to spirit and the true nature of the earth."

Visionary mushrooms, like those Adam showed me, have a long history of use among the shamans of many cultures, and their sacred nature is recorded, as Adam said, in the art of several prehistoric peoples. Mesolithic rock paintings from 8,500 years ago, in Tassili n'Ajjer, North Africa, for example, depict "mushroom shamans" transformed by the power of the plant into the mushroom itself and, through this, able to meet with the spirits to which these plants are a gateway.

"Mushroom stones" (also called "wave stones") have also been found in Wales and in Celtic Ireland, dating from the same period. They stand up to fifteen feet tall and are shaped like giant mushrooms. Scientists believe that these stone sentinels, most often carved from limestone, were caused by erosion from the waves of lakes that have long since vanished. And yet there are many mushroom stones that are found nowhere near water, in Ireland and in other places of the world, such as those in the ruins of Mayan temples in South America and in Mexican sacred caves in Colima State dating from 2,000 years ago.

These holy plants were known to the Mexicans as *teonanácatl*: "god's mushroom." Aztecs called them "genius mushrooms," "divinatory mushrooms," or "wondrous mushrooms." The conquering Spaniards and Catholic missionaries also saw their power and, in their fear of the spirits, regarded their use as pagan idolatry. They had a different name for them: "the devil's mush-room."

According to some sources, the first documented use of sacred mushrooms in England was in 1799 and occurred in London. *The Medical and Physical Journal* described how a man who had been picking mushrooms in Green Park included them in his harvest and served them to his family for breakfast, accidentally trans-porting them all into the spirit world. It was, by all accounts, a happy experience. The doctor who treated the family commented on how the youngest child "was attacked with fits of immoder-ate laughter, nor could the threats of his father or mother refrain him."[17]

None of this was known to me at the time, of course, and so whatever happened next was truly in the lap of the gods.

Adam knelt down and whispered to the mushrooms in an attitude of prayer, then, leaving a drop of mead and a pinch of tobacco at the center of each circle, picked two or three from each grouping, being careful to break their stems and not to dis-turb their roots, until he had a handful, which he placed in his pocket.

"Now come with me," he said.

---

17   From Everard Brande (1799), "On a Poisonous Species of Agaric," *London Medi-cal and Physical Journal* 11 (November 16): 41–44 (as quoted in "Psilocybin mush-rooms" article on http://en.wikipedia.org/wiki/Magic_mushrooms; website is current as of March 24, 2008).

We walked to a darker part of the field, where the shadows of trees and hedgerows made a deeper black, and I noticed a circle of stones that I presumed Adam had laid out earlier. It was wide enough for us both to sit comfortably within it.

"Hold an attitude of reverence as you cross the stones," he said, "and make it your intention—if it *is* your intention—that this will be your first step towards meeting the angels."

We walked into the circle and sat. "Before we begin, I want to tell you a little about these mushrooms and how they help us. They are plant allies with a strong intent to open doorways for us. Once they are eaten, they change the nature of our energy and make us visible to the spirits, who are called through their curiosity to see what these humans are doing in their world.

"Their effect, from the human point of view, is to dissolve us into a more liquid form so our outer and inner worlds blend into one. You will see visions, for example, which may relate to energies you are carrying from past experiences. The spirit of the plants and the angels you call through eating will understand you by these visions because they speak the language of symbols. If you are worthy, they will know it, because these symbols are whispers from your soul to theirs. The correct attitude, therefore, is one of the humble seeker, the reverent, and one who understands that, no matter what you see, feel, or sense, the plants are offering you a healing: an opportunity to divest your soul of sin—or, in straighter words, of the energies that do not serve you and which, if you insist on holding on to them, will lead you into illness.

"There may come a time when you wish to spit or to vomit as these visions unfold, and if that is the case, you should do so. What you give up is an attachment to an unwholesome event from the past and, in purging it, you release the energy of that event so you return to a state of at-one-ment.

"If you maintain the attitude of a seeker, the angels will know your quest for healing and it may be that they will also help you—though there is no guarantee of that—but at least they won't scare you out of your wits!

"My question, then, having explained the risks and the possible benefits to you, is: do you wish to open the doorway? It will be a night of adventure if you do, and you may make new allies for your life which is yet to unfold, or you may experience nothing or be brought face-to-face with your deepest fears. All of these possibilities will enrich your soul, which, by taking this challenge, will find expansion. You are free, however, to make a refusal, in which case we will pay our respects to this place and leave. It is your choice."

There is something in me, I realized then, which will always go forward. Years later, I looked up my family history and coat-of-arms. Its motto is Celtic in origin and it means "I Shall Not

All Die." No matter what the circumstances, that is, there is a tenacity to my blood that craves life, experience, and evolution. I was already half scared out of my wits to be in this strange situation with Adam, miles into the fields in the dead of night and now invited to take a visionary plant and meet the spirits he had described as "angels of the storms" or, in his previous explanation, as giant birds with a taste for flesh and souls. But I would not say no.

Hearing my decision, Adam nodded and counted out eighteen mushrooms for me and nine for himself. "This is your adventure," he said. "I will join you in it only to be present, and I will eat fewer mushrooms because I do not need the same energy as you to enter the doorway. I will hold a space for you here instead and make sure you do not wander too far if I sense that there is danger.

"One final warning: it is best not to leave this circle of stones unless I invite you to do so or it becomes absolutely necessary. Keep your spirit-vision instead and watch what happens without becoming a part of it. The stories you may have read about fairies claiming unwary humans and taking them to their realm for seven earthly years are there for a reason: precisely as a warning to not go too far."

With that, he handed me the mushrooms, and I put them in my mouth. They tasted of dirt, old cellars, decay, and something for which we have no description: as if their sap, the plant-blood I was digesting, was made of electricity and acid.

Adam had assumed my dislike for the taste and offered me a drink from his flask: meddyglyn. I was grateful to receive it.

Nothing happened for a while except a feeling of increasing cold and a desire to shiver, which I put down to the night air, and a tendency on my part to yawn, which seemed nothing unusual given the hour. Adam, however, gave knowing attention to these details.

With the silence and spirit-vision, I also noticed that the field was coming to life. Rabbits played within its theater; a fox, even, walked unhurriedly across it. But these were normal, though amazing, encounters with nature, which are open to anyone willing to see them, and nothing, I imagined, to do with the mushrooms.

Something was different about what I was seeing, though: the fact that I could see it at all. The field should have been in blackness, illuminated only by a cloud-hidden moon, and yet I was seeing more than shapes, as if a luminosity shone up from the ground. I had clearly seen a fox, for example, in all its detail, without that appearing unusual—until I realized that I should not have seen *any* detail.

I looked at the ground to see where the light was coming from and discovered that the grass had itself become liquid and was shimmering and rippling. Trees, as well, looked as if they were bending with the gentlest of breezes, taking the atoms of the air into themselves and blowing them out like wisps of smoke. As I took my attention away from them, trails of light followed my eyes across the field.

I closed my eyes and, from nowhere, there appeared a grid of orange lines, humming and sizzling like an electric cable in rain. It undulated, moving and morphing, swaying and changing, until I felt sick to my stomach with its movements and opened my eyes again to find balance.

The image, however, remained, transposed on the landscape, and behind it another image like a pool with ripples spreading outwards as if a pebble had been dropped into it. Sights became sounds: each image a symphony, butting up against the other in what should have been a cacophony of noise but was actually an exquisite blending. The sounds became one: a high-pitched hum and a lower sound conjoined like the soothing whisper a parent might make to a child. Beneath this was a heartbeat, which I suddenly understood as my own, beating its drumlike celebration of being into the whole of creation, which responded, in the form of this field at least, with a shimmering throb each time the drum was struck.

I was beginning to feel dizzy again, so I closed my eyes once more. This seemed to work, but then an interior journey began.

I noticed, somehow, how the contours of my brain were like the grain of trees; how my out-breath began in my lungs but also in the wind in the trees: all one breath, in and out, reaching into infinity; and how my blood pumped to the sound of the drum that was now everywhere, and was made of water and salt, like the sea or the purging meal of the sin eater. There were connections everywhere and in everything. Less than three percent of my DNA separated me from anything else on the planet or, perhaps, in the universe, and I felt what Adam had meant when he spoke of the need for peace and at-one-ment, because everything then made sense, perfect as it was.

I felt suddenly "enlightened" and laughed at the beauty of life, its unity, mystery, and wonder, and at how we human beings had thrown up great complex structures in the face of its divine simplicity. I had no idea why, but the very action of this realization drew in a chilling darkness. Perhaps my laughter had been irreverent or, perhaps, beneath enlightenment; there was always darkness: a sadness at our lack of understanding of the wonder of the world and our inability to find peace in its mystery.

The darkness coalesced and came together like mist. It took the form of a corpse standing before me, the life drained out of it and its hands reaching out for me. The mushrooms translated its unspoken message, and I understood how easy it is for people to give up on life and become one of the "walking dead," lost in the realms of a life unlived, snaring others with their own sad dreams. I felt a strange mixture of euphoria at a secret revealed, then despair at what that secret might mean—and then laughed again as the corpse disappeared into the earth, and I thought to myself how curious these mushrooms were—sounding exactly like Alice in Wonderland.

A wave of new bliss rolled through me as if my atoms had merged with the air and I was held in a warm glow that was everywhere within and around me. I sighed, and it sounded like angels.

Looking up to drink in more of the beauty around me, I noticed, at the periphery of my vision, shooting stars. No, not shooting: *floating* stars. They drifted in past the edge of my sight and became pulsing lights that hovered before me, then faces rushing towards me in a procession that was so fast it was a blur and, at the same time, so slow that I could study the detail of each. Faces I knew mixed with faces I had never seen and of those I have only seen after that night. Some smiling, some in pain, some contorted, some shining in prayer, sacrifice, or sexual ecstasy. I watched them all with empathy and detachment. After what seemed like hours of this, it stopped abruptly, and the peaceful silence returned.

Then, taking their place before me stood three of the most beautiful beings I had ever seen. Shimmering with light, human

and yet nonhuman, they held out their arms to me. In one movement, I stood and took their hands and felt love flow into my
veins. It found my heart, which exploded with joy, sadness,
delight, wonder, awe—every human feeling all at once.

I stepped beyond the stones to embrace the angels. And then
the world shifted again as I heard Adam cry out "No!" I felt him
grab for my leg, but it was too late. I was already facedown on the
earth, somewhere between ecstasy and terror.

Enough of my mind remained that, hearing Adam's cry,
I reached into my pocket and found the ash wand he had given
me. I jammed it into the ground and held on to it for dear life.

My movement created a new effect, however: the ground I was
lying on became glass, not grass, and I saw beneath me a deep
pit, which fell away into a seemingly bottomless void. Within it,
the orange grid I had seen earlier stretched like a web from side
to side, vast and glowing with energy. I could feel its heat from
where I lay, and I knew that if I touched it, my body would be
fried.

The most worrying thing, then, was that fractures were
appearing in the glass from where I had stuck the wand into the
earth, making movement impossible in case the ground itself
should shatter. All I could do was lie still and watch as new cracks
opened up and parts of the earth fell away.

And then, with a final splintering sound, there was no more ground beneath me, and I fell.

I did everything I could to avoid the fiery grid, trying to twist and turn so I altered my trajectory as I plunged. Mostly I succeeded, but still my right forearm and chest came into contact with one of the threads, which was burning hot and razor sharp at the same time. I saw my arm sliced open, but there was so much heat from the grid that it was cauterized immediately and there was no pain or blood. I still have an inch-long scar on my arm, though, and on my chest where my skin met the web.

At some point in my fall, I felt myself lifted by talons. They pierced my shoulders like hooks, but again there was no pain. I looked back to see one of the angel-like beings I had seen earlier, who was holding me to slow my descent. This being—it is impossible to say whether it was male or female—guided our flight through the web and into the tunnels beneath the earth until we landed in a glade of trees deep within the ground. Mist weaved itself through them like a living thing, coiling around the trunks and boughs like snakes.

The inhabitants of this place—shining immaterial beings, most of them taller than me but some of a child's height—seemed completely unperturbed by my presence. There was a pool before me, hazel trees around it, with six streams running from it in a horseshoe shape, and a number of the beings were busying themselves at this, adding flowers to the water and blowing on its surface. It came to me without words that they were blowing blessings into the water. I felt myself held at each elbow and guided into the pool until I stood waist-deep.

Again without words, I understood that this was a form of baptism, a washing away of the outside world. I sat down and my body was washed for me, and then drops of water were splashed into my eyes ("for clarity of vision"), my ears ("to hear the voice of the earth"), my nose ("for the perfumes of life"), my mouth ("to speak of the wordless"), and onto the top of my head ("for clear thought"), my hands ("for sensitivity"), and my heart ("for knowing kindness"). The six streams leading from the pool were the streams of the senses by which we know the world, the sixth being our intuitive knowledge of God and the soul.

I was released from the waters and dried beneath the sun. I heard the words "sit down" and moved to do so but found I was already sitting. Before me stood one of the light beings, while others made a circle around me. The one in front of me had a female energy but no consistent form: one moment a doe, the next a fox, then a bear or a bird, always returning to light between each of her shapeshifts.

I felt a tickling sensation in my scalp and saw that, from each of the beings around me, a thread of energy emerged and attached itself to my head.

"We do not entertain many visitors from the outside," said the shapeshifter. "Most people, hearing the legend of the simorgh, do not seek us out, and that is the way we prefer it, for we choose our companions carefully. You come with the recommendation of a friend, however, and so for you we have a gift."

At first I thought she meant the bath I had been given but then, rising in tempo and intensity, I felt waves of energy from the beings around me, pulsing along the threads that linked us, carrying information that felt like warmth.

It began slowly but eventually became dizzying, like a huge download. Words, as if written in fire or neon, arced across the sky, along with images, equations, feelings, memories, poetry, incantations, and songs, becoming a white-light blur that left me reeling. I wanted to shout for it to slow down, but at that moment it suddenly ended and, in the calm that followed, I understood, somehow, that all of this information was crucial—as well as completely useless, as if every memory, emotion, and image carried the data of a thousand lifetimes and was so infinite in its implications that I could spend my entire life pondering the meanings of a single thought, and wasting my life by doing so.

Finally, one phrase—*Be Tranquil*—began repeating in my mind, and at the same time shining in the sky before me, where it made the shape of two triangles, one on top of the other, undulating and like mirrors to each other.

Be Tranquil Be Tranquil Be Tranquil Be Tranquil
Be Tranquil Be Tranquil Be Tranquil
Be Tranquil Be Tranquil
Be Tranquil
Tranquil
Be Tranquil
Be Tranquil Be Tranquil
Be Tranquil Be Tranquil Be Tranquil
Be Tranquil Be Tranquil Be Tranquil Be Tranquil

It looked like a chalice, formed from the triangular symbols for male and female, or like a figure of eight—the lemniscate, or symbol for infinity—and it pulsed rhythmically in and out of focus, gradually speeding up to a hypnotic flash of words whose meaning was much greater than this single, simple expression. It meant "accept who you are," "stand in your power," "know your truth," "follow your destiny," "release expectations," "let go," "relax," "embrace," "engage"—all of these things and more. Finally it meant: "We are here for you."

My head buzzed with the information, and I lay down beneath the glow of the words and slept.

I awoke on the ground outside the circle of stones, still holding the ash wand, just as dawn was breaking. The sky was a luminous blue, tinged with gold and orange flames. I lay on my side for a moment, drinking in its perfection.

Standing up, I felt the stiffness in my joints, the ache in my back, and the fuzziness in my head of a man who has slept a long time. Stretching myself and looking around, I saw that the ash in front of me was not a wand at all but a small tree, about seven years old I would guess, and somehow that didn't seem strange, although I knew, of course, that I could not really have been away for seven years, or, in reality, for years at all, merely minutes or hours. My rational mind put it down to the hallucinations I had experienced with the mushrooms and reasoned that I must always have been holding on to the tree. Actually I didn't really care one way or the other. There wasn't any point in caring—or, rather, I felt liberated from care.

"Welcome home," said Adam from behind me. "Well, at least the angels didn't destroy you!"

We offered our thanks to the stones and dismantled the circle before we walked back to Adam's cottage, he with a stick of ash in his hand.

"And what did they teach you?" he asked.

"That some things are important," I said, "but only if we believe they are. And that life is far simpler than we pretend."

"Yes," said Adam. "Those are the truths of angels."

IN SUBSEQUENT YEARS, I would continue my work with teacher plants like san pedro, ayahuasca, and sacred mushrooms, and learn more about how they reveal the fabric and patterns of the universe: the geometry of reality itself.

The shamans of the Amazon, for example, drink a hallucinogenic brew called ayahuasca, which is made from vines and leaves. Those who are artistically called paint their visions onto clay pots and textiles. The shapes and structures they create look like grids of energy much like those I had seen.

With mushrooms, for me and for others who have eaten "the flesh of the gods," these grids are orange, pulsating, and there is no doubt that they are a portal opened by the plants into the nature of true reality: the world of forms reduced to its most primal before the universe becomes nothing but energy. This is reality at its most fundamental, and it is available to anyone through the work of magical plants.

I stumbled upon another coincidence in 1995, when I picked up a book by Malidoma Somé called *Of Water and the Spirit*. In it, he recalls his initiation into the Dagara tribe of Burkina Faso, Africa, one aspect of which was to enter a portal created by tribal shamans into "the world beneath the Earth."

He describes how, entering this energy portal, he

> began to see light. At first it was like an aurora borealis, shot with areas of dark and ones of extreme luminescence—rays of such intensity they made me think of the cosmos in expansion or a cosmogony in progress. The light was so powerful that it would have fried my sight into blindness under ordinary circumstances, but somehow I was able to gaze at the skies of the underworld and survive ...

Very quickly this luminescence changed, transforming itself into countless colors, a symphony of luminescent wires, all in motion and breathing life ... I grabbed the one closest to me ... [and] something interesting caught my attention: the wire of light I held in my hands: a bundle of countless fibres clustered together to form an environment of light waves that reminded me of the Milky Way ... a live bundle in which tiny cells of changing colors moved slowly upward within what looked like a thin tube of translucent glass. Each cell twinkled. They were alive ...[18]

---

18   Malidoma Somé, *Of Water and the Spirit: Ritual, Magic, and Initiation in the Life of an African Shaman* (Arkana, 1995).

10

The Path of Purpose

He climbed toward the blinding light
And when his eyes adjusted
He looked down and could see
His fellow prisoners captivated by shadows;
Everything he had believed was false.

Stephen Dunn,
"Allegory of the Cave"

THE TRIP WE had planned to Wales came round soon enough. We travelled by train from Hereford—a Victorian Gothic station dating from 1856, with a forest green waiting room and hard bench seats—to Llanddewi Brefi, the place of Adam's birth. On the way, Adam entertained me with the legends of Wales, which had a certain Gothic quality themselves, although their history was much more ancient than that.

"The flag of the Welsh is the red dragon—*Y Ddraig Goch*—because once there really were fearsome dragons in Wales. Their origin is unclear, but some say they were snakes reared by witches, which had drunk the milk of a woman and eaten Communion bread, and because of these unnatural acts were transformed into winged serpents.

"They had their lurking places in the many caves of Wales and are remembered by some of our place-names—like Sarffle ('The Serpent's Hole') in Llanarmon-Dyffryn-Ceiriog. These dragons—the *gwiber*—attacked all who crossed their paths. There was just one way to destroy them, and that was to wrap a red scarf around a post into which sharp nails had been driven. The gwiber, driven mad by the color, would attack the post until it bled itself to death on the hidden spikes. But a few escaped, and the children of these serpents still meet on Midsummer Eve to join their heads so that a 'snake ring'—*glain nadroedd*—is formed, which, through their writhing, they cause to slide from their tails. It hardens as soon as it touches the earth and leaves a circle of glass. Should you happen to find one of these rings, you will have good fortune in all your endeavors.

"Some of the dwelling places of serpents—caves and holes in the ground—were used as initiation chambers for healers and holy men, who were placed in these caves, sometimes for days and nights in darkness, before their rebirth from Cerridwen's womb. These tombs are entrances to *Caer Wydyr*—the underworld—a name which means 'Fortress of Glass,' after the rings created by dragons. Caves with wells or rivers close by were the most auspicious for these initiations, because they were fed by water—the blood of Cerridwen, which nourished her life-giving womb."

I knew Adam well enough to understand that he rarely brought up a subject of myth or magic that was unconnected to an adventure we were about to have, and I wondered where his story was going next. Adam seemed in no hurry to make a point, however, and began another seemingly unconnected tale.

The Three Curses of Lleu

LLEU, SON OF Arianrhod, the so-called "virgin-goddess," had a curious birth. When Arianrhod's uncle, the sorcerer

Math, tested her virginity with his wand of chastity, she at once gave birth to Lleu, who was then carried off by her brother, the warrior Gwydyon.

Lleu was reared from that day by Gwydyon, since Arianrhod could not find it in her heart to love her son. Indeed, she tried to kill him, and when that did not work, she placed a series of curses upon him.

The first was that he would never have a name, the second that he could not bear weapons or wear armor, and the third that he would never marry a woman of any race of people. All of these—the giving of a name, weapons, and the right to marry—are the initiations that a mother must bestow upon her son when he comes of age. But instead of wishing him well, Arianrhod had only ill will towards Lleu.

Gwydyon, however, took pity on the boy and tricked Arianrhod into giving Lleu his name and weapons. But the third curse was harder to break. How to find Lleu a wife so he could have children to carry on his name? After much searching, Gwydyon arrived at an answer. With the help of Math, he created a wife for Lleu by magical means: a wife made of flowers, since Lleu could not marry a human bride.

This flower-wife was called Blodeuedd, and at first their marriage went well. It was not long, however, before Blodeuedd fell in love with another—Goronwy, Lord of Penllyn—and betrayed Lleu when he was away at the hunt.

Together, Blodeuedd and Goronwy plotted Lleu's death, but their plans were not so effective, and instead of killing him, Goronwy's magical spear transformed Lleu into an eagle instead.

Gwydyon again came to Lleu's rescue, and finding the boy in his bird-form, he turned him back into a man, whereupon Lleu was able to kill Goronwy with his own spear. He could not find it in his heart to kill Blodeuedd, however, and so as punishment for her treachery she was transformed into an owl, who still haunts our dark woods.

◆ ◆ ◆

"Stories like these are rarely just idle tales, and often they contain insights into human nature and our capacity for sin," said Adam.

"In this case, it is a simple tale of incest. Why else would Arianrhod's uncle be 'testing her virginity' with a 'wand of chastity'? Why would her brother be so quick to carry the child away?

And why would Arianrhod try to kill her son or want to curse him?

"What this story reveals is the sins of family. Lleu had three curses upon him: that he might not have a name—an understandable reaction from a mother made pregnant by incest, and presumably against her will; that he might never carry weapons—the attempt, that is, to keep him weak and incapable of the same violence done to her; and that he might never have a human wife through whom he could carry his identity forward or know the pleasures of the flesh—a reaction, no doubt, to Arianrhod's disgust at her own experience of family.

"Those were Lleu's curses, but, in some ways, we all have such crosses to bear because we all arise from a family drama of some kind, and it is quite common, after all, for parents to curse their children through their actions, inactions, or words. This circumstance is known, in tales like the one I related, as a geis. It is like a ghost in us—something alive but not alive—and it must finally die before we can be reborn.

"Although you and I have not experienced a childhood like Lleu's, you might say that our upbringings have cursed us in some ways, too, to be the men that we are. My experiences caused me to become a healer when I might have wished to be a sailor or a woodsman. Through your experiences, you have decided to become an artist or a writer as a reaction *against* your parents' wishes that you become a lawyer, a doctor, or some other secure professional.

"A curse is simply a limitation of our freedoms, then, and ironically it does not matter whether we accept it, as perhaps I have done, or rebel against it, as you are doing now, because either way we define our lives in terms of it and make its restrictions ours. I became a healer because my parents wished it, and you will become a writer—or a bum!—because your parents do not. The question, then, is one of degree: is our curse so bad that we cannot bear its limitations or are we prepared to live with it?

"Lleu's curse was a bad one, but he faced it head-on and found a way around it. He neither accepted nor rebelled against it but made it his sacred challenge, and in so doing his life became a quest to find power on his own terms—by making magic, guile, and awareness his allies. In this way, he became his own man, true to himself, and what could have been a life of tragedy became an adventure of the highest order.

"Now, you might ask how one recognizes the peculiar challenges facing us and how we develop the awareness necessary to overcome them so that a curse does not determine the limitations of our lives. The answer to that is found in the cave of the dragon, and in ancient times there was a process to help with such matters.

"It was called 'the sitting out.' A young man would go off into nature and lose himself in the hills and then sit with his thoughts for a day and a night, sometimes longer, to ask himself these four sacred questions:

Who am I, really, beyond and beneath the projections—the hopes, fears, dreams, and curses—of my family and others? Who am *I*?

What am I doing here, and how is my life unfolding?

Where is life taking me: am I still on the path of my purpose?

Who will come with me: who can I count amongst my allies to help me meet this purpose, and who must I let go of?

"In the cave initiations I told you of, men would enter Cerridwen's womb—the earth itself—and ask their questions there, seeking answers from Caer Wydyr, the spirit world. This form of the sitting out therefore takes place in darkness and is sometimes known as 'the pilgrimage to the land of the sun at midnight,' where illumination comes from within, not from the world of sights and daylight.

"The final outcome of asking these questions is to forgive those who have cursed us—as an act of love and compassion, if that is possible—in the realization that those who curse others are themselves already cursed. Perhaps, like Arianrhod, they live in the midst of their sins, and deliberately or in fear and ignorance wrap others in the shroud of their shadows. Perhaps, like our parents, their hopes and ambitions for us are the curses they transmit, and this arises, too, from their own fears. Love and compassion for the sinner is not necessary, however; it is only important to be free of their curses so that we, like Lleu, can take back our lives. This is also achieved through forgiveness, because by this action we release our own attachments to the curse that we bear so its shackles no longer hold us.

"We have come to Wales for two reasons. The first is so that you may make this quest for yourself and find your own forgiveness. The second I will reveal to you later."

WE WERE MET in Wales by a man who Adam introduced as Cad—the short form of Cadwalader, a name which, in Welsh, means "leader of the battle." Its short form therefore meant "battle," although Cad looked anything but a warrior or a leader to me. He was slightly younger than Adam, with a sweet and open, weather-worn face, clear eyes, a smiling disposition, and a lively humor. He piled our bags into his car and we set out for his cottage in the hills above the town.

He and Adam obviously had much to catch up on, and over glasses of whiskey made sweet with honey, they talked deep into the night before the fire, long after I had found my way to bed.

Their late night did nothing to prevent an early start, however, and the dawn had barely arrived as Adam and I made our way into the hills the next morning. Cad was nowhere to be seen, though—I thought he was wisely sleeping in to recover from the night before.

At around 10 AM—after, by my reckoning, a four-hour hike—we arrived at a waterfall, one of many in Wales, but this one, according to Adam, a place of special power.

"The water of the holy wells is charged with magic," he reminded me. "But not all wells are visible to the eye. Beneath that waterfall is one such well: a place where nature has carved a pool and where, centuries before the Christian church and its newfangled religion arrived, people would meet to make their prayers and offerings to the Lady of the Waters. I bet if you dived into that pool now you would find a thousand gifts to the spirits. This, where we stand, is a place charged with prayer."

Just beyond the falls was a cave, our final destination, and in front of it, to my surprise, was Cad. He had a fire going, and over it a pot of liquid was bubbling away.

"Have you explained everything to the boy?" he asked as we drew near.

"In a manner of speaking," said Adam.

"You have explained about the cave, then?"

"In a manner of speaking."

Cad rolled his eyes and made a sound that, had he been Jewish rather than Welsh, would have been "Oy vey!"

Sitting me down near the fire, Adam took his cue and outlined his plan for the next few hours. It amounted to no more than I had suspected, given his speech of the day before: that I would be spending the night alone in the cave "in the darkness amongst the dragons," on a quest to find answers to the four sacred questions: *Who am I? Why am I here? Where is my life taking me? Who will come with me?* But first, he added, it was necessary for us to purify ourselves, and this was the reason for the fire.

Bubbling away in the pot were pine needles, the heart-shaped leaves of the linden tree, and the leaves and bark of the birch—*bedwen arian*—which Adam had long ago described as a protector, "the first tree of the old language" and symbolic of new awakenings.

Next to Cad were a pile of blankets that he had evidently brought with him. Stripping to our shorts, all three of us huddled around the fire and threw the blankets over us to make an elementary sweat lodge, and then breathed in the steam and scent of the leaves. The aroma was uplifting and cleansing.

Beneath our shelter, Adam offered prayers to the spirits of the place, to "the angels," and to "God," asking them to bless our undertaking and help me find vision. Cad offered his prayers for my safety and understanding.

We remained under the blanket in semi-darkness, making ourselves pure in the menthol steam for some time before Cad threw the coverings back and we ran to the stream, standing beneath the icy waterfall for some minutes to "wash away sin and be amongst the mermaids."

And then it was time. We dressed and stood at the entrance to the cave.

Adam pulled out his fob-watch and studied it. "Twelve o'clock exactly," he said, "the crucial hour. When the clock is precisely at twelve we are in the place of thresholds, for it is neither morning nor afternoon, and time stands still between the movement of the hands. In that space another world opens, which, if we are fast enough on our feet, we may enter, slipping past the watch hands into a land without time. That is why the hour is crucial: because we must take our opportunities now."

It was not until much later that I learned that Adam's watch had been a gift from his father and had stopped at the moment of his death: twelve o'clock. Adam had never repaired it or even investigated to see if a simple rewinding would start it again. To Adam, it was not a timepiece but a reminder that it is always "the crucial hour."

Adam and Cad stepped forward and began sweeping the cave with bundles of leaves—the same bundles I had seen Adam use during his healing of the village woman all those years ago. It was a cleansing not concerned with cleaning the cave walls or floor but with removing unwanted energies from the air. Cad carried the pot of water and used his bundle to direct purifying steam into the corners and roof of the cave.

"You remember the questions?" asked Adam.

I nodded, and with that I entered the dragon-cave, and the entrance was sealed behind me with branches and ferns. The blankets were thrown over this makeshift doorway, and I stood alone in darkness.

In creation myths the world over there is also a crucial hour: the hour at which new life begins. In these myths, there is darkness before the birth of the human race, and within it an undifferentiated oneness where all is God and everything is one: the unified consciousness or cloud of awareness that Adam had spoken of, and which we read of in the Bible and in the sacred texts of all nations, as well as the sagas and legends of tribal peoples.

> In the beginning God created the heavens and the earth. Now the earth was formless and empty, darkness was over the surface of the deep, and the Spirit of God was hovering over the waters.

Genesis 1:1–2

And then, something happens: this intelligent oneness becomes curious and wants to know itself—*ourselves*, really, since it is our consciousness that makes up this great cloud. It must therefore do two things: it must separate itself into forms so it can look back and see itself for the first time; and it must create light so it can see itself at all.

> And God said, Let there be light, and there was light...
> the first day.

> *Genesis 1:3–5*

And so it is that with illumination comes separation and the arrival of opposites, and the universal consciousness we all once knew is split into many. Ever since that first day, we have been striving to find unity; to return to the community of souls we were born from and to know God again.

To do so, we must enter the darkness once more and experience what it is to be God, as part of a world without forms. It is for this reason that sages and mystics the world over have used caves as chambers of meditation and reflection to reconnect with that first God-consciousness and return to a state of at-one-ment.

In Cornwall, for example, Iron-Age Celtic communities constructed subterranean passages, known as *fogou* ("underground chambers"—a word which derives from *ogo*: "cave") in which their seekers would quest alone; while, on the other side of the world, in Africa, where all human life began, the darkness is held so sacred that it is even forbidden to light candles after nightfall in case protective tribal spirits are scared away. Somewhere, within all of us, darkness holds the answer to our destinies.[19]

In my cave, amidst the ancient spirits and sleeping dragons of the serpent hills, I felt a sense of peace and order, as if I was a part of history, held by a timeless tradition. Not being able to see a foot in front of me, it did, indeed, feel like I was a child of Cerridwen's womb, and, enveloped by the ink-black air, I settled with my back to the cave wall and began my quest for answers.

Who am I?

The Welsh bard Taliesin asked himself the same question after accidentally imbibing a magical brew of inspiration prepared by Cerridwen, the dark goddess, for her son.

Cerridwen's servant, Gwion, had been set the task of stirring this brew for a year and a day in the cauldron of the underworld. At the end of his vigil, however, three drops of the elixir boiled out and scalded his hand, and in licking the drops from his fingers, he absorbed the potent magic.

Realizing what had happened, Cerridwen pursued Gwion; a chase during which they both transformed themselves into a variety of creatures until the goddess, in the form of a hen, finally swallowed Gwion when he became a grain of corn.

---

19 I have written more extensively on darkness practices in my book *Darkness Visible: Awakening Spiritual Light Through Darkness Meditation* (Destiny Books, 2005).

As a result of this, Cerridwen became pregnant and gave birth to Gwion again, but in a new and more beautiful infant form. Disgusted, she threw the unwanted child into a river to die, where he was rescued by a fisherman, drawn by the baby's majesty and luminescence. This "fisher of men" named the child Taliesin ("he of the radiant brow").

Taliesin became a great poet and wrote of his adventures in *Cad Goddeu* ("The Battle of the Trees"), one of the four ancient books of Wales:[20]

> *I have been in a multitude of shapes*
> *before I assumed a consistent form*
> *I have been the narrow blade of a sword*
> *I have been a drop in the air*
> *I have been a shining star*
> *I have been a word in a book*
> *I have been an eagle*
> *I have been a boat on the sea*
> *I have been a string on a harp*
> *I have been enchanted for a year in the foam of water*
> *There is nothing I have not been.*

---

20 See *Sacred Texts, The Battle of Goddeu, Book of Taliessin VIII*, translated in 1868 by William F. Skene. This is available online at http://www.sacred-texts.com/neu/celt/fab/fab029.htm and was current as of March 24, 2008.

He was not one form, Taliesin realized, but a spirit—the essence that flows in all things—and in this he was limitless and free.

The same realization occurred to me now. A thousand projections may have been laid on me, a thousand names, dreams, ambitions, expectations, and labels—by my parents, my teachers, my society, my government, my world, even by Adam himself. But, beyond this, beyond my "name" and "identity," I was nothing—or rather I was everything: anything I wanted to be. It was only my *acceptance* of labels and the definitions of others that made me "who I am now," when, in reality, I was free to be anyone.

This is what Adam had meant, and what I had understood from my encounter with the "angels," of the necessity of letting go of attachments—my attachments to other people's perceptions and to my own. By making a refusal I could be reborn, start again, and choose any identity I wished.

Who was I? "I" was not an "I" at all. I was infinite, unknowable: whatever I chose.

Why am I here?

To live the purpose of my soul; I understood that from my studies with Adam. The fundamental purpose of all living things, he had said, is to love and embrace life fully; to be all that we can be.

My decision, on the day of reading omens with Rachel, was to express my purpose through writing. Now I began to think that this answer was far too simplistic—that rather than bringing freedom, it would be another way of me accepting my geis. My parents, as Adam had pointed out, wanted more than anything for me to have a successful career as a result of their own dreams and fears, and, despite my rebellious nature, as Adam had called it, I had nonetheless defined myself in terms of a job as well, just as they had, instead of embracing the fullness of all I could be.

Life was a sacred challenge, not a limited option, and I had to see it in all its richness, expressing my truth in everything I did—in how I lived—and not just looking at it in terms of "career opportunities." Like Taliesin, I could be anyone and anything I chose.

Where is my life taking me?

My answers so far had raised another question: "What, then, is love?" The purpose of the soul may be to love and live fully, but love has its shadows too. Indeed, it seemed to me that more harm has been done in the cause of misguided love than in the name of anything else—from the witch burnings by the agents of the "one true God," to the ethnic cleansings conducted by "God's chosen" against those who are "not worthy" of love as a result of their color or culture, to the simple neediness of those lovers who, in relationships, demand affection and attention from others while ignoring the pain they cause.

Love was a challenge and not an answer in itself; a quest for truth and wholeness, not a destination to be arrived at; and, if the purpose of our souls is to love, then the answer to my question of "Where is life taking me?" should be "towards truth and integrity." Surely, if I followed that path, then love would find me.

I asked myself if I *had* been moving towards truth and integrity though, and I realized that the answer was no. I had not always been honest with myself or taken responsibility for my actions, and therefore I could not blame others for their mistakes either. Where my life would take me, from now on, I decided, was towards greater compassion.

Who will come with me?

Some people feed our souls—they are "good medicine," we might say—whereas others, when we know our purpose, pull against us or stop us in our tracks. I felt no judgment in this realization since everyone is on their own journey towards the same destination, whether they are being true to their souls or do not even realize there is a path beneath their feet. It is simply that we are at different stages, or indeed may be exploring different paths altogether as we try, at this time and in our own ways, to find the right one for us.

The people I wanted to accompany me were those in whose presence I would receive nourishment and support, and who I could support in turn, because I knew their souls.

But I also realized that to remain exclusively in their company would be another self-limitation because I could not grow and develop without a different perspective to keep me fresh and awake. To only be around fellow travellers would be a form of death, since nothing can exist without its opposite or by finding something to value in everyone. Nature evolves through difference and cooperation.

I understood, then, that I needed *all* the people in my life and even needed to seek out, from time to time, people who opposed my ideas and disagreed with what I stood for. They were my allies in helping my soul to expand through the chances they gave me to test my love and truth.

From this perspective, it was easy to complete the final stage of my quest, which was to arrive at a place of forgiveness. Staring into the darkness, it dawned on me that there was actually nothing to forgive. Just as I had seen in my other encounters with nature, there was no meaning to life, no point, and no sense to it apart from the meanings I gave it. Things just were, people just were; all of us trying to make our way in a world of mystery, alone in the darkness and trying to remember our light.

I could name tens of people—maybe hundreds!—who had harmed me, betrayed me, manipulated or tried to control me. But so what? They were not responsible for their effects on me or for steering me from my path; if I had lost my way as a result of their actions, the responsibility was mine. They would be answerable for their sins (if sins they were), because everything we do has its consequences. My responsibility was for my own sins; for allowing myself to be caught in illusions, influenced by others, and my purpose to be weakened. No one but I could be accountable for that.

Against the backdrop of darkness, I saw all the people I considered my "enemies"—angry, resentful, fucked-up people. I raged at them and spat out a stream of curses—and then I began to laugh. Weren't the first on my list of "enemies" people who were angry and resentful? Their faces were my own.

I had been projected onto and received the curses of others, but I had done my share of projecting and cursing too. The person I really needed to forgive was me.

I allowed myself to embody each of the people I saw before me, to feel how they felt towards me and how they sensed I felt about them; it was exactly the same. In the darkness, it was easy to see the cords of energy between us, binding us together in mutual dislike, perfect mirrors for each other. I set about cutting the ties that bound us and taking my energy back for myself.

Then I wished my "enemies" well, thanked them for their lessons, and let them go. My body relaxed immediately, and I felt a weight lift from my soul.

Throughout the night I revisited the four sacred questions, and I have visited them again many times since. The words I hear most frequently in reply to those questions now are from Shakespeare's *Hamlet*, where Polonius offers advice to his son before his first journey into the world:

> This above all: to thine own self be true,
> And it must follow, as the night the day,
> Thou cans't not then be false to any man.

With the arrival of morning, the cave was opened and sunlight flooded in. Cad and Adam had kept a vigil for me all night outside the cave, and I felt an immense gratitude for that. Now we walked together down to the stream to wash away the darkness.

"It was an auspicious night," said Adam, "so I know you will have learned at least a few things of value.

"Around midnight, the sky was full of stars, and looking up, I saw six tiny lights cross the heavens from star to star. Three of them settled at the star they came to and three moved on to another. Such things are common in the sky when we bother to look up! The star-people making their rounds or—well, who knows?

"For you and for the purposes of our journey, their travels are irrelevant. What is important is the meaning of this as an omen, which, I suspect, is that you were able to leave some things behind last night and to find new destinations and truths that better serve you."

Then he took me aside, out of earshot of his friend. "It is a further part of the tradition of questing that the initiate receives a secret or sacred name when he returns to the flock," he announced. "This is a name symbolic of his new birth, and for the first time in his life, he gets to choose his own, free of the meanings of others—one which speaks *his* truth.

"It is a name kept hidden and rarely made known. This is for two reasons: firstly, it provides a solid core that the initiate can return to, so that no matter how others label or see him, he, at least, always knows who he is.

"Secondly, whatever life he leads—and we must hope it is one of virtue and free of sin—if he *should* find himself called to reckoning and standing before the Devil one day, he can trick the old goat by revealing only his given name, not the one he has found for himself! That way he will never end up in the Devil's register!

"I want to share my chosen name with you now, although I have given you clues to it once before, when we first started speaking of sin. It is B*****.

"And now you may choose your own. Look around you and find a sign in nature: something that sings to your soul and by which you will remember the things that were revealed to you last night."

I took in the forest, the stream, the waterfall and hills, the remains of our fire, the cave, and reflected as well on what Adam had related of "star-people" and travellers. As I did so, a word kept repeating in my brain: H*****.

"Good," said Adam. "You are H*****. Remember it."

11

The Sleep of the Blessed

My death will trigger tears in me,
and I shall mourn my life:
A day annihilated by the way
I fail and sin relentlessly.
O Father God, when will it be
that I can say without a lie:
I live because I do not die?

St. John of the Cross,
"I Live Yet Do Not Live in Me"

Rachel was there, of course, along with family and friends, probably thirty people in all, packed into a tiny cottage room. I stood by the coffin, a corpse-watcher now myself, looking down at the sleeping face surrounded by flowers, as if he was resting in a summer meadow.

"The second piece of business we must attend to is to watch over the soul of a friend," Adam had said on our return from the waterfall. David, the herbalist I had never met but who had been Rachel's teacher, had been unwell for some time and had passed away two days before. This explained the urgency with which we had left Hereford, Cad having communicated David's failing health to Adam over the last few weeks, and finally his passing on the morning we left.

I was touched that, despite the sadness of the event, Cad and Adam had still undertaken their vigil for me and made this their first priority, not even mentioning their sorrow at the loss of a friend. Adam, however, pragmatic rather than wholly poetic for once, explained that this order of things was necessary, because I would be playing a part at David's wake too, and it was therefore important that I cleanse myself and approach the event with a clear heart.

On the first night we arrived, I now learned, he and Cad had not been chatting idly about old friendships but making plans, and more importantly, in Adam's words, "telling the life of a man."

"Telling the life" was a form of confession, he said. It is a practice by which we remember the dead to God, relating the story of their lives in the form of memories and impressions, dwelling on the good, and musing on how the dead person may have committed errors and sins but had learned from them and striven to be better as a result. In this way, Adam said, God would notice their good deeds and overlook their sins so they might be received back into "Heaven."

"Many of our most ancient rituals for the dead continue in one form or another," he said, "even though modern people have forgotten they are practicing them. Look around at any funeral and you will see people telling the life of the deceased in their stories and anecdotes and in their praise for the spirit of the man. Cad and I choose a certain formality around this practice, although it is, of course, enjoyable enough to recall the times we have spent with a friend and drink a glass or two to his enduring soul.

"I hope that one day you, or someone like you, will make my confession and tell my life as well. In this way, our days are not wasted but become of service to others who can learn from us—

our mistakes as well as our acts of wonder—and some of our essence may therefore live on in them. It may be, in fact, that we have more influence in death than in life since people are moved to consider us differently when we are gone, and not to dismiss us so easily but pause to reflect on the meaning we have had for them.

"Another custom you will see at funerals is the laying of flowers. We have forgotten the purpose of this, too. It is because the scent of flowers pleases the nose of God, and as their aromas drift upwards, the soul may be carried with them. White, of course, is the color of purity, which is why funeral flowers are most often white, and this is another appeal to God: to see the deceased in a pure light and take notice of the good he did for others. If you pay attention at funerals, in fact, you will see all human fears, hopes, and dreams represented, and the wishes and purpose of all souls made clear."

My role at the wake was to act as "the witness." Adam didn't explain much more than this to me, only that "when others turn away, you must not."

And so I stood vigil, the corpse-watcher at David's coffin, while others drank and chatted and ate the food of our host.

At a certain point in this celebration of David's life, the energy in the room began to change. Nothing was formally announced, but all the same it was as if everyone was expecting something that had not yet happened and was aware that the crucial hour was close. Discussions began to taper off and the noise of the room became a low hum while the jagged edges of hastily ended conversations were left hanging in the air. No one charged their glasses anymore, and no more food was put on plates.

At a time of almost-silence, there were three knocks on the door. Cad was standing closest to it, and pausing for a moment to look around the room, opened it. During that pause, everyone else turned away from the door and the coffin.

Adam entered, wearing the same clothes as when I first met him, right down his shoeless feet.[21] Only his face was different. It was smeared on one side with ash and on the other with soot.

Both of those symbols I recognized from our time together. The ash was the remnants of all the confessions he had heard during his life as a healer of the soul, including my own—and, I wondered, David's? The soot was the mark of lightning that had struck the holy oak and which, to Adam, represented enlighten-ment, a word that in his philosophy did not mean "divine rev-elation" but simply "making lighter"—an unburdening of sin

---

21 It was often the case that Adam went without shoes, even when walking in the fields. He believed shoes to be unhealthy—a "cage for the feet"—and that it was much better to "touch the earth," to ground oneself, and to "have a feel for the planet beneath us." His views are consistent with those of reflexology, which informs us that areas of the feet correspond to those of the body, and that by stimulating the feet and the 7,200 nerve endings there, it is possible to create health and cure illness. Walking without shoes is therefore an excellent form of "therapy" for the feet and body. It is not, as far as I know, a requisite of sin eating practice, but I do it often nevertheless, and I recommend it to others.

that would otherwise weigh down the soul—although, I suspect, both definitions are ultimately the same.

He walked towards the coffin, with me as his only witness, then leaned over it onto the body, his lips at the dead man's chest.

Barely in a whisper, he began:

> *If we confess our sins, He is faithful and just*
> *And will forgive our sins and purify us*
> *From all unrighteousness.*

(1 John 1:9)

He then started his telling of David's life: all the good he had done, the deeds he had committed in error, and how his soul had been improved by making a refusal to sin in the same way again.

This done, he leaned farther into the casket and began to suck up the air around the corpse so that a soft hiss filled the room. Allowing my eyes to go out of focus, as I had done so many times before in an attitude of gazing, I saw strands of energy curl up from the body and enter Adam's mouth like those I had seen during the healing long ago.

These were the "weights on the soul": attachments to events and energies that might hold the dead bound to the earth unless they were removed. Adam drew them into his mouth and, swallowing them, reached for a glass of water and took a pinch of the salt that had been laid on a plate by the coffin. He ate and drank, and then continued, as if in an appeal to God to notice the now-pure soul of his friend:

> *Search me, O God, and know my heart*
> *Try me, and know my thoughts*
> *And see if there be any wicked way in me*
> *And lead me in the way everlasting.*
>
> (Psalm 139:23–24)

Now he reached up towards Heaven and, in the way I had seen him do before, quietly clicked his fingers three times. He seemed to be pulling at the air above the corpse, as if dragging something unseen into the room, and then, as I looked more closely, a thread of light drifted down from the ceiling while another drifted upwards from the belly of the dead man. Adam caught them both and, knitting them together, began a whispered mantra of "Amen-Amen-Amen [So be it, truly]; Caritas-Caritas-Caritas [Love and wisdom]."

With that, a luminosity arose from David along the thread—the umbilical cord of the soul—and up into the air. It drifted like smoke, steady, shining, and pulsing, through the ceiling of the room until it was gone completely.

Adam stood up and looked across the coffin into the room. He seemed to be addressing everyone present now, not just the dead man or the god to whom his soul would return.

If you do not do what is right, sin is crouching at your door;
It desires to have you, but you must master it.

(Genesis 4:6–7)

The Son of man came,[22] not to be served but to serve
And to give his life as a ransom.

(Mark 10:45)

It is done. He sleeps the sleep of the Blessed.

His sermon delivered, Adam walked to the door, passing Cad, who bowed and placed in his hand three silver shillings. Then he knocked on the door three times and was gone.

---

22 The phrase "son of man" can be interpreted in three ways. Bible scholars see it as a straightforward reference to Jesus, i.e., "the son of God who was given to man." Since the biblical Adam ("Man") was literally the first son of God, however (i.e., the first human being, or first person who was "of man"), the usage here—which I am sure would also have appealed to the sin eater's somewhat irreverent sense of humor—could also have the meaning: "Adam [or I] came not to be served but to serve," which contains an ironic reference to the way in which the community (here with their faces all turned from the coffin) traditionally interacted—or, rather, refused to interact—with sin eaters. The third interpretation, however, is that "the son of man" stands for humanity as a whole—i.e., that we are all the sons (and daughters) of man in the generic sense of the word. The implied meaning, then, would be that we all have the power to help ourselves and each other through "doing the little things": simple acts of love and kindness which serve God's will and ask nothing in return. This interpretation would probably be most in keeping with Adam's own views.

The hush in the room was filled with murmurs as the people turned around and back to each other, but Cad quickly silenced them. There was more to be done.

He strolled to the coffin and stood alongside me, then reached behind him and poured a glass of whiskey. The first of the people stepped forward and took the glass handed to them across the coffin and the body it contained, drinking it down in silence. One by one, the others stepped up and the ritual was repeated: evidence that the body was pure and no lingering energies would enter the drinks consumed.

I took the opportunity to slip away and find Adam. As I suspected, he was kneeling, retching into the earth alongside a plant whose leaves, I imagined, were already turning black from the inside.

THE SEEMINGLY SIMPLE ritual of sin eating masks a number of more complex spiritual maneuvers. Firstly, the action of "eating" from the belly of the deceased—whether the food was actually placed there or alongside the corpse, as it was in this case—is a form of what shamans call "extraction medicine": the removal of energies from the body that would otherwise weigh down the soul or block its progress into the light.

Should this happen, the soul might wander the earth, lost between worlds, as a wraith or hungry ghost, so addicted in its attachments to life that it would be miserable and troublesome to others. In this circumstance, the job of the shaman would be to release the soul through psychopompery: escorting the dead across the threshold of life and death, into the world beyond.

It was hoped that this would never be necessary, of course, both for the salvation of the deceased and for the peace of others. One purpose of the food in sin eating or extraction rituals, therefore, is to absorb the sins of the dead in the knowledge that spirit craves matter and that these energies would be attracted to the stronger life-force of the "living" food than the dead corpse. Once the food was eaten, these energies were removed as a simple consequence.

The food itself and how it was consumed varied according to the sin eater's lineage. Sometimes it was bread and ale, sometimes water and salt. The latter was more useful to the sin eater since, as Adam had explained, salt water is an aid to purging, and the removal of the sins he had consumed would be the sin eater's next priority so that he did not become a "sinner" himself, using the life-force of others as a source of his own power. In another variant, the sin eater would not consume food at all but, more as Adam had done in the earlier healing of the village woman, take the sins upon himself and then rid them from his body by casting them into salt water or burying them in the earth.

Secondly, as the sin eater went about his duties he would be telling the life of the dead man and praying for his soul to enter the kingdom of Heaven. This, in itself, is a form of psychopomp work but also a type of soul retrieval: a shamanic practice for making the soul complete again. Shamans know that trauma, shock, or the presence of sin can cause the soul to fracture so that parts of it become lost. The job of the shaman is to find and return these missing parts and knit them back into the soul that remains.

Through this, God—or Great Spirit, or however the shaman visualizes the great cloud of awareness that is our universe—receives a whole human soul and can thereby recognize and embrace its own missing part in a way that would not be possible if only a fragment remained.

Thirdly, the ritual of sin eating was a community healing and a form of absolution for all of the people at the wake. When a relative or close friend dies, there is often a feeling of guilt on the part of those who live on—we ask ourselves if we could have done more, and why we didn't give love and attention to the deceased while he was alive, when it might have truly mattered to them and to us.

Guilt arises as a result of our perceived sin of neglect, and the ritual of sin eating helps to assuage this, because we can at least now see that the deceased has been helped and healed through our employment of the sin eater.

At the same time, Adam's short sermon, "If you do not do what is right, sin is crouching at your door ... you must master it," was a reminder to those in the presence of death and reflecting on their own mortality that our journeys will all end in the same place one day: we will be in our coffins and awaiting the reckoning of our souls. While we are alive, however, we have choices. Sin is, indeed, ever present, "crouching at our doors," and the first sin is illusion: forgetting our purpose and origin. By remembering who we are and the meaning of our souls—by mastering sin, that is—we can make our choices well and snatch our lives back from the Fates. In this, we seize chance and transform it through acts of free will.

The most paradoxical aspect of the sin eater's life remains the way in which he was treated by the community: as a king and as a leper, as Adam had once put it. His role was central to the well-being of individual souls and to the community as a whole, but he was also ostracized from it. Hence, no one but the witness could look at the sin eater during his duties at the wake, since to the community, the sin eater was unclean.

And yet if this was so, it was because of *their* sins that he took upon himself, never his own. One wonders what these sins were that were so dark that people could not bear to look at them, and if they were that terrible, why they continued in them instead of heeding the sin eater's words to master them and to remember who they were.

Perhaps it is this—the thanklessness, solitariness, and emotional hardship of the sin eater's life, as well as the decline of spiritual belief in our modern cities—which accounts for the end of sin eating and why it is no longer central to our funerary rites.

It does, however, survive in symbolic form. In Ireland, for example, it is still common for the corpse to lie in state in the family home, and at another funeral I was to attend in the mid-1980s, I smiled with recognition as a service was held over the coffin and our host then offered a glass of wine and a funeral biscuit to each guest, handing it to us over the corpse, just as Cad had done with his glasses of whiskey for the people at David's wake: proof that the soul was clean.

Similar practices continue in the English Midlands. In the graveyard of St. Margaret's Church at Ratlinghope, for example—a Shropshire village so small that it was once described as "a bit blowed off a village"—is the final resting place of Richard Munslow, said to have been the last sin eater for that area. Munslow is recorded as having attended funerals and eaten a meal of bread and ale, and then made a speech at the graveside in order to take upon himself the sins of the dead and ensure the peace of the soul so that its wraith did not haunt the village: "I give easement and rest now to thee, dear man. Come not down the lanes or in our meadows. And for thy peace I pawn my own soul. Amen." I do not know the date of Munslow's own death (or if it was attended by anyone who ministered to his soul), but in photographs the grave is ancient, suggesting that the practice of sin eating in Shropshire died with him many years ago.[23] And yet at funerals in this county "burial cakes" are still made, which the guests eat in honor of the deceased.

The same cakes are offered at funerals in Northumberland and in the Peaklands of rural England. They are a sort of yellow bread, quite sweet and spicy, or else a plum cake that is either round or three-cornered, and big enough to be carried under the arm. They are taken with a glass of "burnt ale": warm beer spiced with nutmeg, cloves, ginger, and mace. These practices are relics, too, of the sin-eating tradition.

In the Highlands of Scotland, there is another rite that continues at funerals known as "earth laid upon a corpse," where the deceased is buried with a wooden plate on his chest that holds a small amount of soil and salt. The soil represents the body,

---

23 A photograph of Richard Munslow's grave is available at the Shropshire Gallery website (www.shropshiregallery.co.uk). The direct link, http://www.shropshire gallery.co.uk/towns/ratlinghope/IMG_0270.html, was current as of March 24, 2008.

which will decay and become one with the earth, while the salt represents the soul that always endures.

In other countries, these customs are also honored. In Bavaria, a corpse-cake is placed on the chest of the deceased, which is eaten by the closest living relative as his or her ransom to sin. In the Balkans, a small bread image of the deceased is eaten by members of his or her family for the same reason. In Holland, *doed-koecks* (dead-cakes) are eaten that are marked with the initials of the deceased.

The early Dutch settlers in America's New Amsterdam carried their customs with them and would employ "inviters" (sometimes called "warners") to go from door to door, informing friends and relatives that a loved one had passed on and to ask them to attend the funeral. Along with the invitation, they delivered a bottle of wine, a pair of gloves so that the guests might touch the corpse without fear of spiritual contagion, and two dead-cakes: large biscuits that were not to be eaten but kept in the home as a reminder of the soul that lived on.

Welsh settlers who moved to the Appalachians during the 1700s and 1800s may also have continued the tradition, perhaps in a more original form, at least according to the Reverend Maureen Killoran, who, in 2002, began a sermon with the words: "You may have heard of it, the custom of sin eating—an old Celtic tradition that may still happen back in these mountains."

If it does, it happens quietly and in secret. In a 2007 *San Diego Union Tribune* article entitled "Clean Plate, Clean Soul," Sandi Dolbee wrote that "this apparently now-defunct practice has been traced to the countries that make up the British Isles ... Several scholars of Appalachian history [however], contacted about sin eaters, knew little, if anything, about the practice. If it ever occurred there, it's not going on anymore, according to one of them."[24]

Those who know better also understand that the denial of sin eating as a ritual practice is common. The Welsh website www.nantlle.com—created by local people to keep the history of the Nantlle Valley alive—also carried an article on sin eating in 2007:[25]

> During the nineteenth and twentieth centuries, the majority of historians tended to deny the existence of such a person. As usual, the victors got to write the history, maintaining that the very idea was clear evidence of the ignorance of ordinary folk. How could anyone believe in such an idea, let alone take part in the ceremony in their modern, enlightened age?

---

24 *San Diego Union Tribune*, "Clean Plate, Clean Soul," by Sandi Dolbee, February 3, 2007. This is available online at http://www.signonsandiego.com/union trib/20070203/news_lz1co3sin.html, and was current as of March 24, 2008.

25 Nantlle Valley History, "The Sin Eater." This is available online at http://www .nantlle.com/history-llanllyfni-sin-eater.htm, and was current as of March 24, 2008.

Especially under the influence of the Nonconformists, rejecting the old beliefs was not enough. In order to create an ideal image for the Welsh, according to the standards of the age, they would deny the existence of so many of our old customs, or, worst of all, they would refuse to speak about them at all (this was chiefly in answer to the insulting insinuations which were called "The Betrayal of the Blue Books"—i.e., government reports of the 1840s which gave a very unfavorable view of the state of Wales).

Nevertheless, according to the residents of Nantlle Valley, "Across the whole of Wales and the Borders also, the sin eater had a prominent role in funeral ceremonies."

One local described the ritual of *Coeden Bechod* ("The Tree of Sin") in the parish of Llanllyfni, where the family of the deceased placed a potato that had just been taken from an oven onto the chest of the corpse and left it to cool so that the food would absorb the sins of the departed. It was then put beneath the Tree of Sin, where it was consumed later by the sin eater. A small amount of money was also left there to pay him—"a person shunned by decent folk"—for his services.

"It was most important to give food made from the best ingredients," say the residents of Nantlle, "to ensure that every last crumb was eaten. Hence the practice here in the parish of Llanllyfni of offering a potato in its skin underlines the importance of the wholeness of the gift and its accursed ingredients. Some say that the custom still continues ..."

"DID YOU SEE?" asked Adam as I drew near. I nodded. "Then you did your job well. The task of the witness is to see, so there can be no doubt."

Adam opened his hand and showed me the three silver shillings. "A gift for you," he said, "for the witness.

"These few coins were never the payment of the sin eater—the wage for taking on the sins of others was far more than that—but metal, as you may know, is a perfect conductor of energy, and so it was often the practice to bury these coins away from the corpse as a final guarantee that no sin remained.

"Their function is also to help the healer cleanse his own soul of the sins he has taken on. Wash them in salt water and keep them with you. Hold them in your hand sometimes, during your confessions or reflections—whenever you are in doubt about the ways in which you have acted—and they will bring you back to truth and purify your soul."

I took the coins from him and still have them. Sometimes, in my own dark nights of the soul, I take them out and find some comfort in them.

Adam and I said our farewells to Cad, Rachel, and the others, and caught the train to Hereford the next day. I never saw Rachel again.

Mostly we travelled in silence, both of us aware, I am sure, that we had shared our most profound adventure together, and that the crucial hour had arrived when life would take us in different directions.

I had a place to study philosophy at a university in Birmingham, close to where I was born nearly twenty years before, a cycle completing itself and a subject of study which, without meeting Adam, I might never have considered. Term was starting soon, and both of us knew that I would be leaving to make my way in the world.

Adam, I felt, had also arrived at a final destination. He had never meant me to be his "apprentice" any more than I had wished it. Both of us had simply made ourselves available to chance, but once chance had knocked at his door, he had kept his promises to it and to me. Through our work together, he had also made his confession, the telling of his life. With my imminent departure, he was free to spend the rest of it however he chose.

In fact, I never made it to Birmingham. Chance came knocking at my door again and intervened in the form of an advertisement I happened upon one day for a new course at a college in Northampton, an annex of Leicester University, which would go on to become a world center for excellence in transpersonal psychology: by any other name, the study of the soul.

At this college I could put together my own program of study, and I chose psychology, sociology, anthropology, philosophy, and comparative religion, all of which felt more true to my soul than pure philosophy. I phoned the college and took a place with them.

It was a good decision. For the next four years, in every subject I studied, the words *shamanism*, *soul*, and *spirit* were repeated over and over as we explored the ways of tribal peoples, their wisdom, and their traditional methods of healing.

As a consequence, I had a framework by which to make sense of my experiences with Adam. And so, by chance and free will, are our histories written.

12

Another Garden

The stream will cease to flow;
The wind will cease to blow;
The clouds will cease to fleet;
The heart will cease to beat;
For all things must die.
All things must die.

Alfred, Lord Tennyson,
"All Things Will Die"

I LEFT HEREFORD in 1979 and did not return again until 1984, after my studies were over. In the years in between, my father had died and my friends and I had left university and moved on to marriage, careers, and new locations. I had a "power job" and was living with a woman who would soon become my wife, and our lives were consumed with dinner parties, talk about babies, and strategies for promotions at work. Like most young men, I was absorbed with the ways of the world rather than the ways of the spirit, and I hadn't seen or spoken to Adam since leaving the village all those years ago.

Something, however, did not feel right about my life. The ways of the world that I was giving my time and energy to seemed artificial and of limited importance. I was going through the motions: like everyone else in the 1980s, I was chasing money, fame, and success—and I had no idea why. I think if we were honest, all of the people of my generation, sitting at those vacuous dinner parties, discussing our empty, irrelevant, self-obsessed dramas, would have said the same thing: *we are lost and we don't know where we can be found*. Certainly, my heart was not in this lifestyle, though I could see how its prizes glittered, and I knew that only too easily I could be hypnotized by it and dragged into its sparkling emptiness.

For many people, it was an odd choice for me to return to Ull-ingswick after the bright lights of the city. On the one hand, I had a good job as well as offers to study for a master's degree in San Francisco or for a doctorate at several universities in England. Accepting any of them would have taken me further out into the world, to a place where I could carve a career for myself and get away from this village where time stood still, which is what I had said I wanted for years. On the other hand, I had nothing to really come home for, after all. My choice should have been easy: to move away and "be somebody."

But I was feeling disconnected and restless, and I wanted to regroup, recharge my spirit, and consider my options. To be somebody, I reasoned, I needed to know who that somebody was and what he really wanted to do next.

The "medicine" of the village did not work for me either, though. I slept in, read books, and took walks in the fields close to home, but I generally grew more depressed, listless, and uncertain about what I wanted. The one thing home life did show me, in increasingly glorious detail, was that I was completely lost.

After a few days of "moping around," as my father would have called it, I was even irritated at myself, and I decided to call on Adam to see if there were more adventures to be had or insights to be gained from his more subtle approach to life.

Nothing seemed to have changed as I made my way down the lane to his cottage. There were the same potholes in the road, the same ditches at the side of it carrying the same waste water from the same fields and farms where I had spent my youth. The paint on the doors and windows of the farms I passed still peeled in exactly the same places, their upkeep no better or worse than when I'd left. The trees and bushes seemed the same height, and they had the same birds nesting in them. Even the cattle had the same faces. Time had continued to stand still, and everything was the same.

Until I arrived at Adam's, that is.

There was nothing there. No ramshackle cottage. No garden. No bramble fence and no gate. Instead, the land was clear and flattened, perfectly level and manicured in a way Adam would have hated. I recalled some of his first words to me: "Nature rarely needs a manicure. When we tidy things up, we forget what they are and we try to make them a part of *our* world instead of recognizing the truth: that we are a part of nature. Not *apart*, but *a part*. Every garden is actually a pharmacy when left to its own devices ... and every one of these plants has a purpose. When we chop them down and tidy them up, we deny ourselves their healing."

Adam's garden had been "tidied up," and I knew that he could not be responsible. But surely he must have had some hand in it or given his permission? If so, I was amazed, given his feelings on matters like this.

But there it was: not a brick of his cottage or a plant from his garden remained, and around the land itself was a thin orange wire, the sort that property developers put in place to mark their territory or farmers erect for the same reason before they put up a fence.

None of it made sense. This small plot of land—tinier still, now it was cleared of the tangle of plants that once grew wild upon it—was of little use to a farmer either to plough or for grazing, and of less use still to a developer. And, in any case, no one "developed" in this village. The concept itself was bizarre.

And yet I could not deny what I saw: perfectly level grass, trimmed low, to about an inch or so, and within it wildflowers: bluebells, forget-me-nots, and, in patches, daffodils, as if the land had been recently tended but not cared for. As if, that is, it had a purpose in somebody's plans, but that purpose had not been made clear.

A sudden swell of panic hit me. Like the mystery of Adam's land, my plans were not clear to me either, and part of my reason for being here, with so many confusing possibilities open, and so many misgivings about what to do next, was to gain clarity by returning to what had made sense: the time I had spent with Adam and the learning that had come through him.

But he was nowhere to be seen.

For whatever reason, I found myself staring at the land with spirit-vision—the wide-angle way of looking at the world that Adam had shown me—hoping, I suppose, for some sign I hadn't noticed before so I could understand what I was seeing.

From the corner of my eye, to the left, there was something. Over by the hedgerow that separated Adam's garden from the fields was a single patch of grass that grew wilder than the rest, with daffodils and forget-me-nots in greater profusion. I stepped under the orange wire and walked across the unnatural grass.

Tucked beneath the hedge—I hoped deliberately, though there was no evidence of deliberate intent—was the rough-hewn bowl that Adam had used during his healings, and next to it a clay jar, tipped on its side, its contents spilling out: the ash of all those confessions—my own amongst them—that Adam had heard in his life; some of it still in the jar, some scattered and turned into an alkaline plaster by months or years of rain.

And so at least it wasn't a dream—Adam had lived here. I picked up the bowl and jar and took them with me. There was nothing else, no memento, no message, no other sign I could read.

I asked in the village, of course, and heard theories and speculation—gossip of little substance—as to where Adam had gone, but no one really seemed to know.

Some said he had returned to Wales; others to India or to travel the world. Some, less romantically, said that the council had taken him into care; that he was insane and incapable of looking after himself, so they had intervened by taking his land and, in exchange, had admitted him to an asylum.

Hereford Asylum, at Burghill, was a red-brick monstrosity that I had visited as a helper during my A-levels, when I thought that psychiatry might be another possible career for me—until I had seen that place. I prayed that Adam had not ended up there. But, then, why would he? He had done no harm to anyone, and it was his practice to live a quiet and self-sufficient life. He had not bothered anyone, and there was no reason for others to bother him.

I reminded myself that, despite their liking for gossip, no one in the village could really know what had happened to Adam. None of them, after all, had ever given him the time of day (nor would he ask them for it) when he lived in their community, even if only at its edge, and if people had met him through his healings they would never speak of it or take an interest in his life outside of that.

I realized, finally, that some things are not meant to be known but are better left as mysteries so they may enter our souls as poetry and we can—if we are still and attentive enough—learn from them.

Why some relationships don't work out, why we sometimes allow our parents to die without closing the distance between us, where the people go who, we realize too late, have played their part in shaping our souls: all of these are mysteries for which there are no answers—until we find those answers in ourselves or the day of reckoning comes, when we must hope that all things are finally made clear.

I had no insight into the mystery that Adam had become, and I could only hope that the river that winds through Hereford would carry my question in its wake so that, someday, someone else might find an answer. But secretly I hoped that Adam had found his place, or that he walked with the ghosts of Dunder Camp and, through his philosophy, that those restless souls would find the peace they needed to understand their purpose and move on.

As for me, I finally found a direction, though I would hesitate to say that I found answers. Are there ever really answers until that once-final moment when we look back on our lives and comprehend?

I travelled and sought out healers, sages, and shamans who could help me make sense of the world. And none of this would have been possible without Adam and without my stumbling across his garden as a child.

I realized some time ago that Adam had been more than a teacher to me; he was a friend. It is my sin against him not to have known that at the time, and not to do the one thing he asked of me: to make his confession. But perhaps by this book—the telling of his life—it is one sin I have finally let go of.

The world, even without Adam, remains full of mystery, and it is the job of our souls to explore it: never in the hope of finding answers—or, rather, the one and abiding answer—but staying open to its possibilities, drinking deep of its blessings and the experiences it gives us.

By doing so, we allow our spirits to soar and—just perhaps—we can fulfill our soul's true purpose: to love. Only to love.

◆ ◆ ◆

> May it not even be that death shall unite us to all romance and that some day we shall fight dragons among blue hills, or come to that whereof all romance is but "foreshadowings mingled with the images of man's misdeeds in greater days than these," as the old men thought in *The Earthly Paradise*, when they were in good spirits ...

> *William Butler Yeats,*
> *The Celtic Twilight*

Afterword

Last night, as I was sleeping,
I dreamt—marvelous error!—
That a spring was breaking
out in my heart.
I said: Along which secret aqueduct,
Oh water, are you coming to me,
water of a new life
that I have never drunk?

Antonio Machado,
"Last Night, As I Was Sleeping"

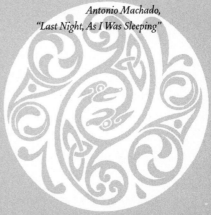

ON A HOT day in August 2007, Ross Heaven and I happened to be driving back to the south of England from a festival in Malvern, Wales. Malvern is only about thirty miles from Hereford, where the story of the sin eater takes place, and so, on a whim, we decided to make a detour and visit the village of Ullingswick, where Ross grew up, and where the cottage of Adam, the sin eater Ross had known in his youth, once stood.

Ullingswick is a pretty little village with an impressive old church and a few farmhouses and residential properties dotted around. As we drove through the country roads, Ross described the village of his youth. Harry's Croft, his childhood home, itself at a crossroads, was now expanded, "developed," and a "desirable middle-class home," in the words a real-estate agent might use, in contrast to the much smaller sixteenth-century cottage that must once have stood there, and the village itself had a sense of aspirational blandness, as if its country ways were being swallowed by the city. Even so, I had a sense of what living there would have been like in the middle of the last century when Ross's story takes place. It was far removed from the urban life I've always led. It felt very peaceful on the surface, but scratch that surface, I sensed, and all things may be possible.

The heat of the day and my emotional reaction to the village made everything hazy and dreamlike. Then, about a mile and a half from the village center, again at a crossroads, Ross stopped the car and showed me where Adam's cottage had stood. His house is no longer there, and as we drove up to where it had been, I could just see a large patch of fir trees, which I imagined the landowner must sell at Christmas time. The land was surrounded by hedgerows, thinned and lower where the gateway to the cottage must once have been. The main approach now was a break in the hedge from the main road.

I wandered onto the land to look around, hoping—like an archaeologist—to find some trace of the mysterious man that Ross has written about. All I found was a piece of agricultural equipment in some overgrown part of what had been the garden—possibly left by the landowner who had planted the fir trees on the site of the old house.

But I wasn't disappointed. Standing on the ground where Adam had lived, seeing the remnants of his overgrown garden and where the house had stood, I got a sense of the character Ross describes in his book. It felt a bit like a pilgrimage and that sense of place that you pick up when you visit the site of past spiritual events, almost like the earth itself retains a memory of what has been.

As I stood, feeling the grass beneath my feet and smelling the sweet scent of hay in the air, I looked back to the main road we had just stepped off of. There, in the distance, was a lightning-struck tree, stark and alone in the middle of the field.

I felt goosebumps on my arm, despite the heat of the day, and knew that I was in the presence of something just beyond the grasp of my rational mind. I could hear whisperings from the past and felt so close to discovering something about Adam and his life that I didn't just want Ross as a conduit to this fascinating old man, the last of the sin eaters; I wanted to know him myself.

Back home in London, I did the typical journalist thing of searching for Adam. When the old faithful of the Internet drew a blank, I got on the phone to Hereford County Council and their archive and records department. The lady on the other end of the phone was a bit perplexed by my queries, as their department isn't usually contacted to find out things this recent, but for a fee they will search at your request.

"You know, it's not guaranteed that we'll find him," explained the lady gently, in case I was related to the person I was hunting for. "There may be parish records if he was active in parish activities."

I suppressed a smile and wondered whether sin eating would have counted as a "parish activity." I couldn't see it making the minutes of parish council meetings. I asked for a search on his name, and as this search is currently taking place, I'm crossing my fingers.

But even if Adam turns out not to be with us any more, I feel like I know him in some way, and by seeking him alone perhaps I have also gained some redemption.

TANIA AHSAN
London, August 2007

◆ ◆ ◆

TANIA AHSAN IS a journalist for *The Guardian*, *Metro*, *The London Paper*, and several mind-body-spirit magazines in the UK.

The Sin Eater Workbook

THE FOLLOWING EXERCISES are offered if you would like to try some of the techniques and approaches in this book. Note that there is no particular structure to be followed in the sense that any one of these practices must be mastered before others are attempted.

❖ Nettle Allies

In chapter 2, Adam remarks that "the spirit of the nettle is a good one—an ally to human folk. Its job is to fight off bothersome spirits who want to take our power away. It will do that for you if you ask it, and any problems with the blood will then clear up. As a bonus," he added, almost in a stage whisper and with a sparkle in his eyes, "it is one of the best plants a lady can use if she wants a bigger bosom!"

Nettles (*Urtica dioica*) are a good source of iron, calcium, and folic acid, so they are excellent for breast-feeding mothers and will help milk to flow (giving you "a bigger bosom" indeed).

They have also been used as a blood purifier and can help in the treatment of anaemia and excessive menstruation, and an infusion of the plant is useful in stemming internal bleeding. Rheumatism, hay fever, and skin complaints such as eczema are other conditions in which nettles have helped. They are also good as a general tonic and will fortify your body if you are feeling run-down.

Nettles can be boiled and eaten like spinach, added to soups, or prepared as a tea. If you'd like to explore their powers, start by picking small, young leaves (they grow bitter with age). Grip them with a firm hand and it is unlikely you will be stung. "Like love and most things in life, the nettle only hurts when you touch it too lightly. When you commit to it, it commits to you. Of course, you'd better ask its permission first—and know when to let go as well! In plain language: grab the nettle firmly, and it will not sting."

Wash the leaves and put them in a pot, adding enough hot water to just cover them. Boil until the water becomes slightly green, then remove them (or leave them in for longer if you prefer a stronger, slightly more bitter taste).

Nettle tea is good served with honey and sliced lemons, and the lemon has a magical effect: it will change the color of the tea from green to bright pink by altering the acidity of the water. Kids love this, and by sharing the tea and the magic with them, you'll be restoring their souls as well.

◆ ◆ ◆

❧ Tree Gazing

In chapter 3, Adam speaks of the importance of trees as "the great transformers" who take our pollution and give us back pure oxygen. They are the lungs of our planet.

Trees are also the great wisdom-keepers because they have been around far longer than us and are connected directly to the earth; they are not "surface walkers" as we are. To learn from trees we must move at their pace, which is much slower than we are used to.

Find a tree that calls to you and approach it by walking towards it "at the pace of nature," paying close attention until you feel a change in the air around you. Then sit down in front of it.

"Most people move too fast to notice that change. But it's always there. It is a change in the nature of things ..."

Allow your eyes to go slightly out of focus as you gaze at the tree, and take deep, slow breaths. Don't *try* to achieve anything in particular; just relax and look at the tree.

After a while, it may be that the tree starts to shimmer, as if it has a glow to it. At that point, ask any questions you need answers to and listen for a response in the form of symbols, images, or poetry that bubble up from your dreaming, non-rational mind.

◆ ◆ ◆

❧ Knowing Your Purpose

In chapter 4, Adam talks about "the four orders of man" and remarks that "there is a web of dreams and a web of lies that we can give our energy to. One will take us home and one will leave us hanging. So, you see, to be truly alive in this world—to do no harm and to fulfill your soul's purpose so you move closer to love—you have to know what that purpose is."

His suggestion for discovering soul-purpose was to do something "seemingly at random" because "the abstract, ambiguous, or absurd carry our meanings" more than "the things we carefully plan and commit to."

My solution to "embracing the meaningless" was to sit by a stream and gaze at the patterns that moonlight makes on water. Yours may be different.

The key thing, though, is to do something unplanned and take pleasure in it, knowing it has something to teach you. Embrace the moment. Sit with it, slow down, relax, and breathe deeply. Then ask yourself: "How is this reflective of my life?"

What patterns does it reveal to you?

What themes run through the patterns?

And what is nature teaching you about
what you came here to do?

◆ ◆ ◆

❧ REMOVING NEGATIVE ENERGIES

Chapter 5 is about a healing I once witnessed between Adam and a woman who had come to him for help, and my realization, in the end, that "the three causes of illness or 'sin'—energy imbalance, soul loss, and spirit intrusion—all arise from *origin*al sin: our belief in separation."

The physical, emotional, mental, or spiritual pains we carry are whispers from spirit that we have forgotten who we are and are somehow out of balance.

Shamans work with these "spirit whispers" by scanning the body and tuning in to (or gazing) at the pain itself. Often our tendency is to sublimate, ignore, medicate, or push away our pains. The shaman's view, however, is that illness is a messenger and can be an ally or guide to us.

To learn from your body in this way, lie down, relax, and gently scan yourself from head to toe, taking your attention to each area in turn. Whenever you meet an ache, pain, or a place of stress or resistance, sit with it and ask what it is there to teach you about the way you are living or the things you could do to make life easier or better for yourself. What is it you need to know?

Thank each messenger in turn and make a commitment to yourself that you will follow its advice (it is in your own best interests, after all), then let go of each pain and your attachments to it, releasing it "to the willows, to the oak, to the clouds, to the flowers of the fields and hedgerows."

From now on, you can use this approach to help you live a more balanced life.

♦ ♦ ♦

❧ Cleansing the Soul

In chapter 6, after witnessing a healing performed by Adam and being exposed to some of the energies in the room, Adam provides a "cleansing tea" for us both.

"This is a blend of herbs," he says, "chief amongst them hyssop, with vinegar and honey. It is not an entirely pleasant taste—though more so than some others—but its job is not to be pleasant. It is to restore balance to the soul by removing residual energies and opening the patient to grace."

If you would like to try this for yourself—if you've had a bad day or been exposed to unwholesome energies and feel "unclean" or "stressed out" as a consequence—the formula is as follows:

Hyssop (*Hyssopus officinalis*): 1 teaspoon dried leaves

Coriander (*Coriandrum sativum*): ½ teaspoon dried herb

Rose (*Rosa* spp.): ¼ teaspoon dried petals

Rue (*Ruta graveolens*): A pinch (⅛ of a teaspoon or less)

Vinegar: 3 dashes

Honey: 1 (or more) tablespoons, depending on taste

Add all of the ingredients[26] except the honey to about a pint of water and bring gently to a boil, then simmer for ten minutes. Strain and decant the liquid, and add the honey. Drink while warm.

The key ingredient, hyssop, is known as the "holy herb" because of its ability to bring healing in whatever form it is required. It is an aid to greater alertness, for example, but is also relaxing and good for treating nervous exhaustion. (Coriander has similar properties for the relief of anxiety and insomnia.)

Hyssop has also been used to treat lung, nose, and throat congestion. Externally, it can be applied to bruises to reduce swelling and discoloration, and one old country remedy for cuts sustained in the fields is to apply a poultice of bruised hyssop leaves and sugar to reduce the risk of infection.

Hyssop leaves can also be added to soups, salads, and meat dishes. They have a strong, slightly bitter, minty flavor.

◆ ◆ ◆

---

26 Rue is known as the "herb of grace," and brushes made from it were traditionally used to sprinkle holy water at the ceremony preceding High Mass. It should be avoided, however, if you are pregnant, as its main physical effect is on the reproductive system, and it has been used historically to decrease fertility and lower sex drive (in men and women) and to promote abortion. Its use in this mix is symbolic rather than essential.

❖ The Art of Dreaming a Nature Ally

In chapter 7, Adam reveals that "every healer must make an ally in nature before any healing can be done. This ally is your first contact with the spirit world and will act as your guide, your ambassador, and your emissary. Through it, you will be introduced to the world of nature and find other allies who can assist you in many ways."

Adam's suggestion for finding this ally was to dream it: to approach sleep with deliberate intention, that is, by going for some hours without sleeping and then setting a purpose for your dreaming self: *to meet a guide from the spirit of nature who will help me with my quest and the purpose of my soul.*

To intensify the dreaming, Adam made me a "Celtic dreaming bed" of ferns and a "pillow" of moss and stone which, in all honesty (and no doubt unsurprisingly), was not all that comfortable.

A better solution, if you have the luxury of time and want to avoid neck and back aches, is Lucy White's "Healing Herb Bed" (in Zoe Hawes' *Herbal Journal*, published by Pomegranate Communications Inc., 2006):

"The inspiration for the healing quilt was to go to bed and wake up healed," she writes. "The mattress and pillows are stuffed with sweet, fresh hay mixed with lavender and meadowsweet for a deep, relaxing slumber."

If you don't want to stuff your entire bedding, sleep with a "dreaming pouch" of hay, lavender, and meadowsweet.

Another alternative is simply to sleep outside on a sunny day, preferably close to a stream or other running water, which was a traditional practice among Celtic bards for receiving inspiration. As with all dreaming work, it is your *intention* that is key.

◆ ◆ ◆

❧ Omens from Nature

"The way to receive these signs is to put oneself in the place of the betwixt-and-between," says Adam in chapter 8; "on the threshold between worlds where the spirits whisper loudest to us. This form of divination is called *rhamanta*—omen-seeking from nature—because nature, you see, is the visible face of spirit and will reveal the truth to us. All we need do is listen and have faith in what we are told."

The practice for taking guidance from nature in this way "is to walk out with a question in mind and let it be answered for you." Find a betwixt-and-between place: the threshold of a forest, the bank of a stream, a gateway, the edge of a shadow—"whatever place sings to your soul"—and ask your questions there.

You will need three such places so you can check and double-check your answers and so the wisdom of nature deepens in its precision.

When you have found your places, close your eyes and turn around three times as you ask your question, then open your eyes and look around. Whatever you see first is the augury you are to receive.

Write down what you are told each time and then use your imagination, as the Celtic diviner did, to create a single story that links all three symbols together.

Dream yourself into this story, and see what it tells you about your life.

◆ ◆ ◆

❧ Ways of Seeing the World

There are many ways of seeing, Adam explains in chapter 9. The first and least useful is normal sight, where, in the case of most people, we miss 90 percent of what is right there in front of us.

Gazing is a different way of looking at the world, where the foreground and background are deliberately reversed, and it is therefore possible to see the things we normally overlook or take for granted.

Then there is spirit-vision: "wide-angled perception," where awareness is taken to the periphery of our sight so we give more attention to what we see out of the corners of our eyes, which is the area from where all visual spirit communications and manifestations first appear.

The last "attitude of seeing" is focusing: narrowing the eyes to study something at close range.

These three ways of seeing are all useful techniques for merging with nature and opening ourselves to its spirit.

The way to explore and develop these new skills of vision is as follows:

1. Close your eyes and stare into the darkness as if you are looking at a real scene. This is *focusing*: bringing the eyes into an attitude of *seeing with intent*.

2. From there, soften the eyes into *gazing*, which also means slowing the breath and relaxing into the scene.

3. Then allow your eyes, still closed, to widen into *spirit-vision*. This feels like a curtain opening and takes you deeper into the scene.

4. Finally, open your eyes and look at the world around you with a wider and more relaxed vision, so you are *naturally* attentive to the detail in front of you and to your sides, without being focused on anything in particular or overly concerned with any of it.

5. This leads to *blending*, so you become one with the environment, and it is moving through you as much as you are moving through it. You become *a part* of nature, not *apart* from it.

◆ ◆ ◆

❧ SITTING OUT

"It was called 'the sitting out.' A young man would go off into nature and lose himself in the hills and then sit with his thoughts for a day and a night, sometimes longer, to ask himself four sacred questions."

In chapter 10, Adam explains the Celtic vision quest, a process for exploring who we are and coming to terms with ourselves. Practically, it is simple enough: walk out into nature and find a place where you will not be disturbed for at least a day and a night. Take little or nothing with you—no mobile phones, notebooks, or other distractions—just a bottle of water, warm clothes, and yourself. Have a question in mind, then sit and watch nature and the flow of the world for your answers.

The four sacred questions are:

1. *Who am I* beneath all the projections of others, including those I have bought into myself and which now form "my identity"?

2. *What am I doing here?* Does my life have purpose, passion, and meaning for me, or am I "going through the motions" or living a lie?

3. *Where is life taking me?* Knowing my purpose, can I honestly say that I am true to it—or is there something new, different, and decisive that I must do?

4. *Who will come with me?* Who are my true friends—the ones who will help me to find or meet my purpose, who will support and love me and not ask for my treasure so they can take it for themselves, or for my darkness so I become a pawn in their dramas? Who is it time to let go of?

When you have your answers, leave the place of your questing and make your commitments to change.

◆ ◆ ◆

❧ Confession

"Adam stood up and looked across the coffin into the room. He seemed to be addressing everyone present now, not just the dead man or the god to whom his soul would return: *If you do not do what is right, sin is crouching at your door; it desires to have you, but you must master it.*"

In chapter 11, Adam delivers a sermon to a congregation in Wales who are present at David's funeral, imploring them to "do what is right."

Few of us know "what is right." Life is a mystery, and we all stand alone. It is perfectly possible to think we are doing right or helping another person, but because we live in our world and they in theirs, what we believed was a helpful gesture or a loving word can be interpreted as exactly the opposite. The truth is that there is no "truth," and every one of us really knows nothing.

To cleanse our souls of "sin"—the energy of negativity—in this uncertain world, Adam therefore recommended confession as a self-healing approach.

The simplest way of doing this is to write down what you regard as your sins against others or against yourself.

Write in a stream of consciousness. It doesn't matter whether you intended to do wrong, or even if—in the whole scheme of things—you actually did no wrong; whatever springs from your pen is a message from your soul about a weight you are carrying nonetheless.

Whether it is rightfully yours to carry or whether you are carrying it for another makes no difference. Learn from it, and let it go. If it is a "real sin," resolve to do better. Carrying it further, however, will not help you or anyone else and provides no at-one-ment for anyone.

Reflect on what you have written, and make your resolutions for the future. Then burn the paper, dig a hole, and bury the ash. Walk away, and leave it behind you. This is a form of purging. Having done so, you have a new future ahead of you.

◆ ◆ ◆

A Note from the Author

Each thing exactly represents itself,
and what has preceded it ...
The truth includes all, and is compact,
just as much as space is compact ...
All is truth without exception;
And henceforth I will go celebrate
anything I see or am,
And sing and laugh, and deny nothing.

Walt Whitman,
"All Is Truth"

MOST OF MY books are nonfiction and relate techniques and trainings I have received during my travels and explorations with healers and shamans from many different spiritual traditions. A few years ago, however, I helped someone else write a book.

As it was presented to me, this would be a semi-fictionalized account of the protagonist's "initiation" into a particular form of shamanism, a form for which there is no historical evidence or proof. I agreed to help, believing the book to be a "teaching story" rather than a wholly factual account and that those parts of it based in fact would be genuine.

When the book emerged in print, however, the person for whom I wrote it forgot that it was not wholly from his pen or that it was partly based in fiction. Instead, it had metamorphosed into a "wholly authentic" account of his initiation into a "little-known tradition" and was offered up for—and won—an award for "spiritual nonfiction."

Because of that experience, I want to offer a word or two about what is fact and what is fiction in this book.

First, let me say that the substantive facts of this story are true: there is an Ullingswick and a Harry's Croft and I did move there as a child. Dunder Camp was nearby, and the myths of Hereford are accurate.

It is also true that there was a cottage at the edge of the village, owned by a man who had been a sin eater. From him I learned the healing possibilities of plants and the ways of the soul.

There have been some changes to the story, however.

Firstly, I have altered the names of some of the characters in this book, but without changing their impact on me or the nature of my encounters with them. There was a Rachel, for example, and a David, and the events of their lives and mine unfolded more or less as I wrote them, but Rachel and David were not their only names. Those who loved them (as I did) know who they are.

There was also a Cad—although, by the nature of writing (because he was a part of our story and we were less a part of his), I have not allowed all of his interests, abilities, or magical talents to shine quite as brightly as I could. Cad and I met again and he had other teachings to impart, so perhaps I can make amends for that in another book.

Some dates and timings have also been changed in order not to disturb the flow of the narrative, but the events that took place were real.

Most of all, though, I must make my own confession that, in revisiting these events, I have, of course, had to explore their meanings for me from the perspective of a man instead of a child.

I was perhaps eight years old when this story began, around twenty-four when it ended, and of course our views on things change.

I now live in a very different world. What was an adventure to a child became a quest for understanding to a young adult, and now to me it is an example of Celtic shamanic practices that may still exist around us if we only know where to look. All of these perspectives are still current and true in me, but to deliver a book that has meaning, I have had to present one narrative.

This is the nature of truth, as Adam explained it: that the events of our lives stay the same, but the meanings we give them and our attachments to them are always open to change. My attachments have changed, and I cannot guarantee that everything now is just as it was then. Still, a core of truth runs through this book, which I hope your soul will recognize.

Whatever its truth, or whatever "truth" is, I offer you this book as a work of semi-fiction, because even though its spirit and its message are true, the events of my life are not yours and "the truth," in terms of "what happened," is an individual thing.

If my story helps you make sense of your life, it has done its job. How you put that into practice is where your own story begins.

Index

LLEWELLYN ORDERING INFORMATION

 Order Online:
Visit our website at www.llewellyn.com, select your books, and order them on our secure server.

 Order by Phone:
- Call toll-free within the U.S. at 1-877-NEW-WRLD (1-877-639-9753). Call toll-free within Canada at 1-866-NEW-WRLD (1-866-639-9753)
- We accept VISA, MasterCard, and American Express

 Order by Mail:
Send the full price of your order (MN residents add 6.5% sales tax) in U.S. funds, plus postage & handling to:

> **Llewellyn Worldwide**
> **2143 Wooddale Drive, Dept. 978-0-7387-1356-4**
> **Woodbury, MN 55125-2989**

Postage & Handling:

Standard (U.S., Mexico, & Canada). If your order is:
$24.99 and under, add $3.00
$25.00 and over, FREE STANDARD SHIPPING

AK, HI, PR: $15.00 for one book plus $1.00 for each additional book.

International Orders (airmail only):
$16.00 for one book plus $3.00 for each additional book

Orders are processed within 2 business days.
Please allow for normal shipping time. Postage and handling rates subject to change.

THE WAY OF THE LOVER
Rumi and the Spiritual Art of Love

Ross Heaven

The revered words of Jalaluddin Rumi—the greatest love poet of all time—have endured for centuries. His moving verses can help us answer life's greatest questions: What is true love? How can I be more loving? How can love help me grow spiritually?

Drawing on Rumi's writings, Sufi teachings, and shamanic techniques, Ross Heaven presents an utterly unique spiritual guidebook to love and relationships. Your voyage through every stage of the soul is aided by the Medicine Wheel, a spiritual compass that will guide you on "The Path of the Heart." Use this powerful tool to revitalize relationships, uncover fears, resist self-defeating impulses, recover from depression or "soul fatigue," and master the "Art of Love."

978-0-7387-1117-1 • 7½ x 9⅛, 240 pp. • bibliog., index • $16.95

Va-Va-Voodoo
Find Love, Make Love & Keep Love

Kathleen Charlotte
Foreword by Ross Heaven

How many professional therapists can put together a powerful mojo bag or an intoxicating love perfume to attract a mate? As a relationship counselor and a Voodoo initiate, Kathleen Charlotte offers the best of both worlds in her refreshing, witty, and magical guide to this crazy little thing called love.

Va-Va-Voodoo introduces five key Voodoo Lwa or "angels," including Baron, the spirit who loves spicy rum and cigars, and La Sirène, an ocean goddess of seduction and sensuality. Readers learn how to "feed the spirits" and request their help in attracting a lover, finding "the one," keeping a relationship steamy, or recovering from heartbreak. A perfect blend of practical magic and inspiring, down-to-earth advice, this one-of-a-kind book includes magic rituals, charms, aphrodisiacs, and spells, as well as helpful relationship tips regarding communication, self-esteem, intimacy, sex, break-ups, and forgiveness.

978-0-7387-0994-9 • 7 x 7, 168 pp. • $14.95

TO ORDER, CALL 1-877-NEW-WRLD
Prices subject to change without notice

To Write to the Author

If you wish to contact the author or would like more information about this book, please write to the author in care of Llewellyn Worldwide and we will forward your request. Both the author and publisher appreciate hearing from you and learning of your enjoyment of this book and how it has helped you. Llewellyn Worldwide cannot guarantee that every letter written to the author can be answered, but all will be forwarded. Please write to:

Ross Heaven
^{c}/₀Llewellyn Worldwide
2143 Wooddale Drive, Dept. 0-7387-1356-4
Woodbury, MN 55125-2989

Please enclose a self-addressed stamped envelope for reply,
or $1.00 to cover costs. If outside U.S.A., enclose
international postal reply coupon.

Many of Llewellyn's authors have websites with additional information and resources. For more information, please visit our website:

HTTP://WWW.LLEWELLYN.COM

THE SIN EATER'S Last Confessions